Reflections on America

REFLECTIONS ON AMERICA

Tocqueville, Weber and Adorno in the United States

Claus Offe

Translated by Patrick Camiller

polity

First published in German as *Selbstbetrachtung aus der Ferne: Tocqueville, Weber und Adorno in den Vereinigten Staaten* by Claus Offe © Suhrkamp Verlag, Frankfurt am Main 2004

This translation first published in 2005 © Polity Press

The publication of this work was supported by a grant from the Goethe-Institut.

Polity Press
65 Bridge Street
Cambridge CB2 1UR, UK

Polity Press
350 Main Street
Malden, MA 02148, USA

ISBN: 0-7456-3505-9
ISBN: 0-7456-3506-7 (pb)

A catalogue record for this book is available from the British Library.

Typeset in 11 on 13pt Berling Roman
by Servis Filmsetting Ltd, Manchester
Printed and bound in Great Britain by MPG Books Ltd, Bodmin, Cornwall

For further information on Polity, visit our website: www.polity.co.uk

Contents

Abbreviations

DiA   Tocqueville, Alexis de, *Democracy in America*, 2 vols. [1835, 1840], 1945

DoE   Horkheimer, Max, and Theodor W. Adorno, *Dialectic of Enlightenment*, 1986

ES   Weber, Max, *Economy and Society*, 1978

GARS   Weber, Max, *Gesammelte Aufsätze zur Religionssoziologie*, 3 vols. [1920], 1988

GAWL   Weber, Max, *Gesammelte Aufsätze zur Wissenschaftslehre*, 1968

GPS   Weber, Max, *Gesammelte Politische Schriften*, 2nd edn, 1958

GS   Adorno, Theodor W., *Gesammelte Schriften*, 20 vols., 1997

PE   Weber, Max, *The Protestant Ethic and the Spirit of Capitalism*, 1958

SSP   Weber, Max, *Gesammelte Aufsätze zur Soziologie und Sozialpolitik*, 1988

Acknowledgements

This little book is based upon the Adorno Lectures I gave at the Institute for Social Research at the University of Frankfurt in November 2003. The occasion provided a welcome opportunity to revisit the institute in the close academic neighbourhood of which I began my career forty years ago. It also gave me the chance to revisit the writings of three classical authors in the work of whom some common threads and themes are to be discovered and who propose alternative ways of how we can make sense, to the extent we still can, of the notion of 'the West'. Helpful suggestions have been provided by David Abraham, Harald Bluhm, Christian Brütt, Axel Honneth, Martin Jay, Hans Joas, Peter A. Kraus and Anson Rabinbach, as well as my graduate students Julien Deroin, Nicole Dolif, Dominik Sommer and Robert Schwind at Humboldt University.

Claus Offe
Berlin, 1 March 2005

It is not, then, merely to satisfy a curiosity ... that I have examined America; my wish has been to find there instruction by which we may ourselves profit.

Alexis de Tocqueville

1
Introduction

Towards the end of 2002, when Axel Honneth did me the honour of inviting me to give the Adorno Lectures of 2003, it might already have been foreseen that relations between Europe and America would define the current intellectual and political debates. In choosing my theme, however, I had no intention of involving myself in current affairs, and I would like to hold to that decision, even if not in a completely consistent manner. My academic teaching has already concerned itself with Max Weber's largely unclarified relationship to Alexis de Tocqueville[1] – to whom he was clearly indebted for many of his ideas or actual concepts, yet whom he never once mentions – and with the subterranean relationship of Adorno and the so-called Frankfurt School to Weber's sociology and diagnosis of the times. There are also a few things to be discovered about the intellectual legacy that links Adorno to Tocqueville (who was widely read among émigrés of the 1940s in 'German California'), not the least being the latter's surprisingly developed theory of a 'culture industry' in the 1830s. I therefore welcomed the opportunity to shed some light, if not on a continuity and contemporary elaboration of common intellectual themes,

[1] See Hecht 1998.

then on thematic affinities and divergences that the three great social scientists display, from their different temporal vantage points, in their analyses of a common object, the United States, as well as in the questions they raise about the condition of Europe in their time. The object of these lectures is the disturbing special case of the American model of Western modernization in contrast to European social conditions and the dangers and prospects of development in store for the continent.

To be more precise, the common theme of our three travellers is the precarious fate of liberty in modern capitalist societies. 'Tyranny of the majority', 'iron cage of dependence', 'reification' and 'administered world' – these are the well-known formulas they used, at least in some parts of their work, to characterize the negative destiny of Western modernity, while constantly searching for counter-forces to halt its advance or even to change it for the better. The road to serfdom is the theme they all pursued, for an observation period amounting to no less than 120 years. They saw in America a highly ambiguous combination: both the emergence of a society of free and equal individuals, and its tragically misdirected outcome, which presented itself to them as a system of imperceptible and therefore all the more effective (or anyway inescapable) constraints that took its toll on liberty and ultimately also on equality.

The task I set myself in these lectures was therefore to reconstruct the contrasting self-descriptions and sociological diagnoses of contemporary Europe that arose out of, and as a result of, their trips to and inside the United States.

If, by 'trip', we understand a temporary change of residence with the intention to return, then we may describe as trips all three of these stays in the United States (however different their causes and circumstances). All three are equally governed by a comparative perspective on the European place of origin. These self-perceptions from afar belong to Alexis de Tocqueville, Max Weber and Theodor W. Adorno; their trips took place in 1831–2, 1904 and 1938 respectively, with roughly two generations between Tocqueville and Weber and one more generation between Weber and Adorno. They stayed in the United States for nine months (Tocqueville), thirteen weeks (Weber) and eleven years (Adorno), for reasons that could not have been more different from one another: in Tocqueville's case to conduct study and exploration on the instructions of his government department (the French justice ministry); in Weber's to accept an invitation to a conference, followed by a tour; and in Adorno's to escape from Nazi Germany and to find work in the field of the social sciences.

The three travellers were following a certain intellectual tradition when they set foot on American soil – a tradition in European social theory going back to the late seventeenth century, for which the nature of European problems and the range of possible solutions were to be understood through their reflection in the realities of America. Asia and, especially, Africa were felt by Europeans to be alien regions, and as such the objects of a detached interest in exotic conditions completely different from their own. It is true that America also displayed traces of the exotic in its indigenous peoples, and in the structures and traditions that had been largely destroyed in the process of colonization. But its settlement by Europeans and its share in the Judeo-Christian religious tradition gave it the status of a more or less distant relative whose independent destiny, though perhaps of interest because the welfare of kith and kin was at stake, inevitably also irritated us – and challenged us to make comparative assessments – because of its evident deviation from European patterns.

'America' – both here and there the customary term for the territory of the United States – has for Europeans always been not an exotic growth but a branch on the same tree. But how is it that this branch bears such unfamiliar blossoms and fruits? America provokes a question that makes no sense in relation to Asia or Africa: whether over time we will become like them or they like us – and, if neither, how the persistent differences should be explained and evaluated. We cannot describe America without describing ourselves as Europeans – whether as more or less similar variants of 'Western' society, or as a configuration of contrasts. Observation of the American social experiment has always been a cause for reflection and self-interpretation concerning European identity.[2]

Since the late seventeenth century, it has become customary in Europe to approach the society taking shape in North America as though in a time machine. In 1690, in connection with his contract theory based on natural rights, John Locke wrote: 'In the beginning all the world was America.'[3] And, according to Kamphausen, 'in the eyes of the Old World, America really brought about a new beginning in world history', offering to Europeans the model of a 'natural' social evolution that stretched from the first settlers, as hunter-gatherers, fur-traders and stockbreeders, down to intensive agriculture, industrialization and urbanization.[4] With this time machine it was possible to travel in both the past and the future. It was possible in the past since the relatively short and transparent history, from the first settler communities in the wilds of nature to the gradual formation of a federal and democratic state system of the USA, was simply claimed as a model of development. That which, in Europe, lay hidden in the mists of a long untraceable past could be read as from an open book in the case of the United States. 'Only by becoming Indians can [the settlers] survive in the colonies; they must return as hunters and gatherers to the first developmental stages of humanity, followed by fur-traders and stockbreeders and the growth of intensive agriculture down to industrialization and urbanization.'[5] This conceptual model has defined the American sense of identity down to the present day. It has often been pointed out that many Americans still have great difficulties with the idea that any citizen in any other country could ever opt for economic, cultural or political conditions

---

[2] Kamphausen 2002, 146f.

[3] Locke 1988, 301 (§49, and cf. §108). In the frontispiece of Hobbes's *Elementa Philosophiae* (1642), *libertas* is already presented as synonymous with the state of nature, through the image of 'a woman wielding a spear and bow and wearing no more than a grass skirt' – 'an obvious allusion to the savage natives of America' (Münkler 1993, 46).

[4] Kamphausen 2002, 169f.

[5] Ibid., 169.

and values that are not at least similar to those of the United States, whose validity Americans claim to be 'self-evident'.[6]

If the differences between the USA and Europe are arranged on the temporal axis, we may say, rather schematically, that there are four possible answers to the question of how Europe and the United States relate to each other. The first answer, popular on both sides of the Atlantic in the nineteenth and twentieth centuries, involves one of two evidently incompatible models of the United States: either (A) an *advance guard* whose explorations allow Europeans to gaze into their own future, or (B) a *latecomer* society standing at a stage of development that Europe has already paced out, a kind of 'immature Europe'.[7] In each case, a difference that is found to exist may be given either a *positive* (1) or a *negative* (2) interpretation. The 'positive advance guard' (A1) interpretation claims that in America a technological, democratic or other advance has an origin that we Europeans have only to reproduce, while the 'positive latecomer hypothesis' (B1) states that in America energies and resources already exhausted among us Europeans still have a salutary effect. On the other hand, a negative evaluation leads to the claim that in America certain fateful trends have already gone so far that to look across the Atlantic is not only to see a window on the future but to stare into an abyss (A2). Finally, the fourth variant maintains that America is stuck at a developmental stage of raw, unbridled, uncivilized and destructive infantilism, which 'we Europeans', by virtue of our own experiences and achievements, have already overcome and sublimated in the form of civilization (B2). Linked to hypothesis A1 is Europe's admiration for progressive democratic America, for the mentality of the New Frontier, which is always there to be redefined and conquered anew, with the moral energies of a

---

[6] In the American Declaration of Independence of 4 July 1776, the thirteen participating states famously proclaimed: 'We hold these truths to be self-evident, that all men are created equal, that they are endowed by their Creator with certain unalienable Rights, that among these are Life, Liberty and the pursuit of Happiness.'

[7] Kamphausen 2002, 145.

liberal, individualist, democratic, egalitarian and anti-statist *American creed*. Hypothesis B1 is associated with the theme of a vigorously youthful formation free of the sclerotic burden of tradition from which the Old World suffers;[8] A2 with the terrifying vision of an unrestrained technological, economic and military rationality; and B2 with the collective damage due to socialization in a society without a history, trapped at the level of raw and permanent childhood.[9] Not surprisingly, it is the first two hypotheses that form the basis of America's sense of identity vis-à-vis Europe and its missionary thrust – in the name of civic religion or, simply, religious fundamentalism – to free the world of its ills; whereas it is the last two hypotheses that are the inspiration for many variants of European anti-Americanism.[10] In B2, a major role is still played today by the idea of the New World's 'civilizational immaturity'[11] and denunciations of Americans as 'equality boors' (Heinrich Heine).[12]

---

[8] In an often quoted poem from *Zahme Xenién* (1827), Goethe wrote that America 'has it better than our old continent', because 'in your lively age you are not troubled within by useless memories and futile strife' (Goethe 1958, 9.248).

[9] In his vehement critique of America in the *Lectures on the Philosophy of History*, Hegel compares the relationship of Europe and America to that between Hamburg and Altona, a suburb of immigrant tradesmen (1956, 82) that is nevertheless like a reborn 'expression of a foreign life' (ibid., 87). The settlers have not yet carried America to the level of a rational state – 'the state was merely something external for the protection of property' (84), involving 'respect for law' without 'genuine probity' (85). As to religious life, Hegel notes the prevalence of 'unseemly varieties of caprice', 'the splitting up into so many sects, which reach the very acme of absurdity', and the 'unbounded licence of imagination' resulting in a lack of the 'religious unity which has been maintained in European states' (85). In political life, too, the necessity for 'an organized state' has not yet made itself felt (86); rather, 'the community [arises] from the aggregation of individuals as atomic constituents' (84). Hegel's picture of Americans as depraved half-savages therefore clearly belongs to type B2 and has been an important source and referent for modern 'anti-Americanism'.

[10] Diner 2002.

[11] Kamphausen 2002, 150.

[12] Cf. Diner 2002, 49ff.

2
Alexis de Tocqueville or the Tyranny of the Middle Class

The Versailles deputy judge (*suppléant*) Alexis de Tocqueville, at the age of twenty-five, together with his friend and colleague Gustave de Beaumont, applied to the French minister of justice for a study trip to the United States, with the purpose of investigating its reputedly progressive penal system. The two applicants intended to produce a report that would provide guidelines for reform along American lines, given that the French penal system, with its high rate of recidivism, was considered to be a 'school of crime'.[1] Like many applications for research or study trips today, this one was, shall we say, motivationally overdetermined. The study of prisons[2] was, at least for Tocqueville, a pretext,[3] connected with far broader interests and the hope of laying a foundation for his own political and literary career.[4] The trip was approved, but a ministerial order later reduced its length to nine and a half months, from 11 May 1831 to 20

---

[1] Jardin 1988, 91ff.
[2] Appearing under the title 'Écrits sur le système pénitentiaire en France et à l'étranger', in vol. 4 of the *Œuvres complètes*. Extracts also appeared in German, Berlin 1833.
[3] Jardin 1988, 93.
[4] Pisa 1984, 63.

February 1832. The route of the journey – undertaken, together with his friend and professional colleague Beaumont, on horseback, by coach and by steamer – extended over the states of the northeast, Canada, and the Great Lakes region, as well as the Midwest, which at the time represented the frontier of settlement, and the southeast and the South down to New Orleans in the formerly French state of Louisiana.[5] The strictly empirical research methods Tocqueville used in both volumes of *Democracy in America* were the same as the ones still used today for regional studies: interviews with experts ('I have endeavoured to consult the most informed men'),[6] secondary analysis of statistics, participant observation and documentary analysis, enhanced by reading of political-theoretical and historical studies of the place under investigation.

The condition of the United States interested Alexis de Tocqueville very explicitly[7] not for its own sake but because he was convinced that it offered conclusions, predictions and solutions for an age that Europeans were about to confront: the 'democratic' age. 'It appears to me beyond a doubt that, sooner or later, we shall arrive, like the Americans, at an almost complete equality of condition . . . my wish has been to find there instruction by which we may ourselves profit.'[8] Every word of praise that Tocqueville bestows on American democracy is at the same time an often unconcealed lament for the backwardness of contemporary France and Europe. The obverse is also true: what little there is to criticize in America, what remains to be feared in its future, is cultural-aristocratic balm for the wounds of a European self-consciousness suffering from post-revolutionary turbulence. From this Europe-centred observation of America, with his thoughts constantly turning 'to our own hemisphere' (as he

---

[5] The similarities between this itinerary and the one Max Weber would choose seventy-three years later are striking.

[6] DiA, 1.16.

[7] DiA, 1.3.

[8] DiA, 1.14.

puts it right at the beginning of the Introduction),[9] the author as foreign visitor enjoyed a double advantage (one that also deserves to be made use of in today's comparative studies): foreigners with their 'alien' vision – i.e. a vision more easily 'alienated' or detached from conformist pressures in one's own society[10] and its peculiar cognitive conventions and self-understanding – not only see more than do local inhabitants; they also find it easier to gain the trust of their informants, who, because the stranger will soon leave and no longer be able to make detrimental use of the information, tell him things they would prefer to withhold from local interlocutors.[11]

The author's proposed 'new science of politics'[12] for the age of equality is based on three theoretical variables: the factual *conditions* (historical, geographic, demographic, etc.), the *institutions and laws*, and the *subjective dispositions* marked by both of these (i.e. the customs and sentiments, expectations and norms of the participating actors). Among these variables there is, for Tocqueville, not only an interaction but also, as we shall see, a hierarchy of explanatory power. For Tocqueville, who in this respect is a forerunner of Durkheim, the most important factor in determining development lies in 'customs', not in objective conditions or institutions.[13]

---

[9] DiA, 1.3.

[10] 'No writer . . . can escape this tribute of adulation to his fellow citizens. The majority lives in the perpetual utterance of self-applause, and there are certain truths which the Americans can learn only from strangers or from experiences' (DiA, 1.275).

[11] DiA, 1.16.

[12] DiA, 1.7.

[13] The dark fear with which at least one of the author's multiple selves observes Europe in the present also shapes his later work, especially his *Recollections*, written in 1850–1, which first appeared in 1893. He worries about whether the development of 'customs' will keep pace with the (democratic) change of institutions – knowing well that the customs of the past no longer offer a firm foothold but have fallen into 'ruins'. '[P]laced in the middle of a rapid stream, we obstinately fix our eyes on the ruins that may still be descried upon the shore we have left, while the current hurries us away and drags us backward toward the

Tocqueville is a master of ambivalence, dialectical reversals, simultaneous observation of both sides of the coin – and in this unprejudiced social-scientific skill, with its abrupt changes of perspective and even self-contradictions,[14] he is unequalled by either of the other travellers to America whom we shall consider later. For didactic purposes, it perhaps makes sense to imagine that, in the diagnostic analysis of the age in both volumes of the America book, behind the name of Tocqueville there is an entire collective of authors,[15] whose individual members attend to their subject from various points of view and in pursuit of different arguments with divergent goals, each in turn taking the lead in formulating individual sections of the text. In this book, which is, so to speak, co-authored by the components of a multiple self, we can recognize Tocqueville the aristocratic moralist, Tocqueville the radical democrat, and Tocqueville the detached political sociologist testing out causal explanations.

For Tocqueville, the novel democratic form in the United States represents, in the first instance, not a material gain but a formal loss. He means to say that American society is *lacking* a structural principle that has always operated in the Old World, even though he is convinced that there too it has no future. This principle is that the political rights and duties of individuals are *unequally distributed* and *acquired by birth*. Tocqueville is a theoretician of the 'democratic age' as well as of the conditions and consequences of the political modernization process; but, at the same time, he is far from adopting

---

abyss' (DiA, 1.7). The correspondence of this picture to the vision of the Angelus Novus in Walter Benjamin's 'Theses on the Concept of History' is worth noting: 'The angel', writes Benjamin, 'would like to stay, awaken the dead, and make whole what has been smashed. But a storm is blowing in from Paradise and has got caught in his wings; it is so strong that the angel can no longer close them. The storm drives him irresistibly into the future to which his back is turned, while the pile of debris before him grows toward the sky. What we call progress is *this* storm' (Benjamin 2003, 392–3).

[14] Elster 1993, 107, 112ff.

[15] Holmes 1993.

as his own a normative principle such as popular sover-eignty.[16] As the scion of an aristocratic family, whose members were personally threatened by the events and con-sequences of the French Revolution,[17] he had since child-hood formed the conviction that the major tendency of world history, established many centuries before, was increasingly to erode 'natural' (hereditary) inequalities grounded on a status order of corporate privilege. Alexis de Tocqueville des-ignated as 'democratic' those societies in which the charac-teristic of hereditary and unequally distributed political right was completely lacking or even – the distinctive feature of the United States – had never existed at all. Where no one was born with the privilege of legislative authority, all were equally free to determine the content of the laws. In this respect, democracy in America was not, in his eyes, the product of a revolution so much as the consequence of a structural defect in American society, precisely the absence of a hereditary status order. Almost throughout his America book, Alexis de Tocqueville is free of any restorationist impulse to defend this absent status order as such – precisely because he regards its decline in Europe as irreversible and even 'a providential fact'.[18] He is much more interested in the consequences for human liberty[19] of the growth in equality.[20] He is not interested in how democracy has been able to

---

[16] His own anti-democratic reactionary views are clearer in the *Recollect-ions*, written twenty years later, than in *Democracy in America*.

[17] Jardin 1988, 7f. One of Tocqueville's great-grandfathers died by the guil-lotine in 1794.

[18] DiA, 1.6.

[19] By 'liberty' Alexis de Tocqueville, in the tradition of the eighteenth century and with 'pre-libertarian' emphases, means the opportunity of a political community to practise republican self-government. The oppo-site is 'tyranny' or 'despotism', both marked by the centralization of gov-ernment and power in the hands of an aristocracy or monarchy, and is synonymous with the negation of that capacity for self-government. This concept of liberty is as fundamental to *Democracy in America* as it still is to his late work, *The Ancien Regime and the Revolution*. On Tocqueville's political theory and his concept of liberty, see Wolin 2001, chap. 19.

[20] DiA, 1, Introduction.

advance, but only in how the (anyway irresistible) tide that is washing away the aristocratic status order, in Europe too, can be channelled and steered so that the disastrous results of anarchy and/or despotism can be avoided and liberty can thus be preserved. In answering this question, which we may also regard as the first question of political sociology in general, Tocqueville takes conditions in the United States as a test case. We may formulate the guiding question of the America book like this: how is it that in America an order based on equal human freedom leads quite clearly to prosperity and stability, while in Europe even the first steps on the road to such an order end in war, civil war, continual instability, reactionary regression and constant fear of revolutionary uprising by the popular masses? Or, in social-scientific jargon: under what conditions can the associative, non-hierarchical self-coordination of a complex society succeed, and what can cause it to fail?[21] The puzzle that Tocqueville sets out to solve is, in his own plain words: 'How comes it, then, that the American republics prosper and continue?'[22] The second part of the first volume of *Democracy in America* begins with the assertion, directed at European readers, that 'it can be strictly said that the people govern in the United States'[23] – a pronouncement which, for the contemporary European reader, could only create the expectation that the author would from then on be reporting the horrors of anarchy and mob rule.

Yet just the opposite is true. Tocqueville's conclusion is that the *transition* to democracy, not democracy itself as an achieved condition ('steady state'), is unleashing this destructive dynamic. Liberty, Tocqueville finds, 'is most formidable when it is a novelty',[24] because then the citizens have not yet had the opportunity to live in an 'apprenticeship of liberty'[25] to learn the complementary customs and *habitudes*,

---

[21] See Jardin 1988, 152.
[22] DiA, 1.246.
[23] See the title of book I, chap. 9, 180.
[24] DiA, 1.192.
[25] DiA, 1.257.

but rather continue with patterns of behaviour learned under a pre-democratic regime. America, in contrast, by a divine stroke of luck, is an exceptional case in which liberty came into being without mediation, that is, without a transitional process of liberation,[26] and equality likewise emerged without the violent dispossession of privileged classes.[27] The privilege of having no history, denied to Europeans, means that Americans are in the unique position of having had no infancy but being 'born in man's estate'.[28] This allows them to enter into a stable and virtuous cycle which Europeans have not yet achieved and which, in any case, they will never be able to achieve *in the same way* as Americans.[29] This virtuous cycle[30] consists in a mutual strengthening of institutions, on the one hand, and, on the other, the customs, attitudes, habits, cognitive perceptions and incentives they have brought into being – in sum, the famous 'habits of the

---

[26] 'The great advantage of the Americans is that they have arrived at a state of democracy without having to endure a democratic revolution, and that they are born equal instead of becoming so' (DiA, 2.108).

[27] The pointed distinction between transition and 'steady state' explains why there has been renewed interest in Tocqueville's writings since 1989. Cf. e.g. Galston 2000.

[28] DiA, 1.328.

[29] The European path to liberal democracy, impeded by a pre-democratic history, cannot therefore be the same as the American. In the United States, democracy exists 'by default', that is, because of the absence of centralized rule or status hierarchy. Citizens in the course of their everyday lives must therefore discover and learn the habits and practices that allow them to make the best of this hierarchically unstructured situation. In Europe, on the other hand, we have to acquire the basic principles of democratic political life reflexively and to study them. In Europe the people have to be *educated* to the practice of freedom, and the 'reform of customs' is itself a political task, which in America is unreflexive and, as it were, picked up along the way. In Europe, as not only Tocqueville but also Weber and Adorno believe, the *demos* must be educated 'to' democracy, while the American people are educated 'by' democracy (which exists and to which there is no alternative), so to speak, by osmosis. See Jardin 1988, 222–3.

[30] 'Democratic institutions are shown to generate beliefs and aspirations that, in turn, support those same institutions' (Elster 1993, 102).

heart' as well as of the mind; then, the 'formative' effects released by these institutions in turn help to make those institutions an established and unchallenged fact of life. The author is obviously operating with a theory of endogenous preference-formation, in keeping with the proverb that 'appetite comes with eating' and cannot simply be reduced to an immutable 'hungry' human nature or other external conditions alone.

To illustrate the constancy of Tocqueville's theoretical perspective, I would like to cite as an example of this dynamic model his analysis of freedom of the press.[31] As Tocqueville says, he is investigating the formative effect of full freedom of the press: he is exploring 'the direction which [freedom of the press] has given to the ideas as well as the tone which it has imparted to the character and the feelings of the Anglo-Americans.'[32] We can paraphrase Tocqueville like this: as we in Europe know from our own political situation, the relaxation of censorship, even the introduction of full freedom of the press, is something akin to dynamite in political life. Freedom of the press, as soon as it is established, is immediately used by oppositional forces to spread subversive and revolutionary ideas among the people, to foment political hatred and to undermine the existing authorities.[33] Yet the authorities can use censorship only to suppress the printed word, 'the body of the thought',[34] not the thought itself; the more they fall short of their goal, the more radical will thought become – the familiar European dialectic of a self-intensifying repression, which finally leads to complete despotism. In that respect, the refusal of freedom of the press

---

[31] These remarks on reception studies, the sociology of the media and of knowledge, compressed into a dozen pages and written by a young man of twenty-nine in 1834, are quite comparable in their analytic power to the voluminous writings of today's social scientists who work on these themes.

[32] DiA, 1.188.

[33] 'Woe to the generations which first abruptly adopt the freedom of the press' (DiA, 1.196).

[34] DiA, 1.189.

and the practice of censorship are, from the point of view of the rulers themselves, not only dangerous 'but absurd'.[35] America, with its complete freedom of the press, is 'perhaps, at this moment, the country of the whole world that contains the fewest germs of revolution', and 'the press does not show the same destructive inclinations as in France.'[36] How is this to be explained?

Tocqueville's answer is that freedom of the press in America has always existed, so there has been no need to struggle for it – and therefore it has never been 'new' in that dangerous way. The greater the number of newspapers, the more limited is the power of any single one.[37] Because of the large number of publications, readers become desensitized: they are not 'affected by . . . deep passions'.[38] Because of the cacophony of opinions, they take note of the contents only with a certain detached indifference, which in turn means that the papers hardly attempt to 'form . . . great currents of opinion'[39] but instead offer their readers mainly anecdotes, news and advertisements.[40] In contrast to France, publishers and editors, in their own business interests, refrain from 'discussing the great interests of the state'.[41] Completely

---

[35] DiA, 1.190.

[36] DiA, 1.191.

[37] 'It is an axiom of political science in that country [the USA] that the only way to neutralize the effect of the public journals is to multiply their number' (DiA, 1.193). This is an application of the principle that Madison, in particular, puts forward in *The Federalist Papers*: namely, that it is possible to fight against an evil, and turn it to good, by increasing its dose and spreading it more widely – for example, to fight against social fragmentation by insisting on the division of powers and various 'checks and balances' (*The Federalist*, no. 10). Elster paraphrases Tocqueville: 'The ills of democracy can be cured by more democracy' (1993, 104). This clever idea – that a higher dosage turns a poison into a cure – may be found throughout the history of the theory of American pluralism and democracy.

[38] DiA, 1.192.

[39] DiA, 1.194.

[40] Ibid.

[41] Ibid.

unrestricted freedom of the press also leads to a dispersion, in space and time, of the potential for danger – and therefore defuses it: 'there is scarcely a hamlet that has not its news-paper',[42] and in the press market there is constant coming and going, because the establishment of new papers is always possible and in no way limited by licences or restrictions. On the other hand, no single newspaper but the press as a whole makes the 'chief opinions which regulate society' tenacious and ineradicable.[43] Everything that is uncontentious in the various publications establishes itself in public opinion as 'invincible prejudice' and 'unreflecting convictions'.[44] Readers adhere to 'unreflecting' conviction (which is there-fore immune to objection) not so much 'because they are sure of its truth as because they are not sure that there is any better to be had.'[45] In comparison with this atheoretical,[46] habitual and therefore tenacious pattern of thought or under-lying conviction (one might also call it ideology), 'material interests' are certain beyond doubt. Always and for everyone there is 'a truth which is self-established, and one which is needless to discuss, that "you are rich and I am poor".'[47]

So far, the good news. It asserts that (entirely against European experience and the fearfulness conditioned by it) the same freedom of open communication can result in a completely stable condition, as long as customs and habits are adjusted to these institutions and citizens have become habit-uated to the formative influence of these institutions and the moral principles associated with them – just as freedom of

---

[42] DiA, 1.193–4.
[43] DiA, 1.195.
[44] DiA, 1.196.
[45] DiA, 1.197.
[46] Cf. Tocqueville's constant emphasis on the 'atheoretical' character of political thought in the USA in DiA, 2, part 1, chap. 4: 'Why the Americans Have Never Been so Eager as the French for General Ideas in Political Affairs', and chap. 10. For the category of 'habit' (*Gewohnheit*) in democratic theory now, see, for example, Hartmann 2003 – though without reference to Tocqueville.
[47] DiA, 1.197.

the press conditions the reading public to indifference and orients their thinking to the realities of civic life. Similar good news appears in Tocqueville's considerations on freedom of association, the franchise and self-government. '[F]reedom of association in political matters', he maintains, 'is not so dangerous to public tranquillity as is supposed . . . After having agitated society for some time, it may strengthen the state.'[48] The logic of his argument is the same for all freedoms, even if it is true in political matters that an 'intelligent despotism'[49] will reach wiser decisions than an elected government. But, from a dynamic point of view, it turns out that frequent elections (and freedom of the press) give voters the opportunity to improve their judgement, and elected officials as well as potential candidates have an incentive to achieve at least a minimum of competence for office. He sends his European readership a message which we may freely render as follows: 'It will be all right. We have to go through this!' 'The great advantage of the Americans consists in their being able to commit faults which they may afterwards repair.'[50] The competence of citizens and officials develops in the course of endogenously generated learning processes, and the result is a spontaneously developed intelligence among the citizens that is eventually not inferior to that of an 'intelligent despot'. Another formative effect of democratic institutions is that they teach citizens to interest themselves 'in the welfare of their country'; the patriotic civic spirit is 'inseparable from the exercise of political rights',[51] as if it were a cognitive-motivational residue or echo. Democracy likewise disposes citizens to law-abidingness, by constantly making it clear (a) that ultimately they have made the laws themselves, and (b) that they can change them at any time – a case of stability through contingency reminiscent of Luhmann's system theory.

[48] DiA, 2.126.
[49] Quoted from Jardin 1988, 156.
[50] DiA, 1.247–8, 258. Cf. 443.
[51] DiA, 1.252.

Tocqueville thinks he can also detect such learning processes in the freedom of party formation and party competition, which seems so dangerous from the European point of view. This is due, in his terminology, to a development from 'major' parties, those based on a fundamental ethic of conviction, to 'minor' parties, which act pragmatically and contend for power without a political creed[52] – a perceptive early contribution to the sociology of parties that included a special emphasis on 'Jacksonian Democracy' and would later be taken over by Weber in many details.[53] The characteristic issues in dispute between such parties are ill-suited to promote 'conviction' – or 'class hatred' – and 'to a stranger [appear] incomprehensible or puerile';[54] 'the differences of opinion are mere differences of hue.'[55] In relation to freedom and the destabilizing effects so feared by Europeans, the author sounds the all clear on every front.[56]

But this does not at all eliminate the intrinsic dangers and destabilizing potential of democracy. That is the bad news.

---

[52] DiA, 1.182. He concludes that 'It must be acknowledged that the unrestrained liberty of political association has not hitherto produced in the United States the fatal results that might perhaps be expected from it elsewhere' (201). This is so also because fundamental political and moral conflicts are outside party life and are embodied in separate political associations which are dedicated to themes such as the maintenance of protective tariffs or the regulation of alcohol use. These are also an example of the Madisonian solution according to which the best way to neutralize the disruptive dangers of conflict is to multiply the institutional means of conducting it (202). This idea was later taken up by Lipset (1981), with his thesis that *multiple* 'cleavages' are a decisive prerequisite of democratic stability. A further benefit of the freedom of association for Tocqueville is that it averts the danger of conspiratorial secret societies (202–3).

[53] ES, 1443–8, 1458.

[54] DiA, 1.185.

[55] DiA, 1.204.

[56] The only reservation in this positive judgement becomes apparent when the author (later French foreign minister), not without a hint of aristocratic nostalgia, criticizes the political elites in democracy. He considers them – partly as a result of a disappointing personal meeting with President Jackson – mediocre, ordinary, erratic and therefore poorly

The danger comes not from political freedom or freedom of the press or the freedom of party competition but rather from economic equality and the universal striving for it. The relationship of tension between freedom and equality can easily be decoded as the relationship between *citoyen* and *bourgeois*, between politics and economics. In opposition to his conservative contemporaries, Tocqueville argues that (as the example of press freedom demonstrates) the threat is not that freedom may bring about anarchy but, on the contrary, that equality may bring about despotism. 'The evils that freedom sometimes brings with it are immediate; they are apparent to all, and all are more or less affected by them. The evils that extreme equality may produce are slowly disclosed.'[57] They show themselves when the despotism of commercial life and an equality transferred to political life destroy civic liberty.

In what follows, I shall briefly mention Tocqueville's outline of the way in which self-destructive powers gain the upper hand in democracy and lead to a relapse into despotism or tyranny. As we shall see, he also finds the remedies to this self-destructiveness in the American practice of democracy itself.

The absence of a previous hierarchical structure – in other words, equality – first of all has effects on economic life: it introduces an insatiable greed among people as economic agents. Tocqueville is obviously not talking here about *actual* equality of wealth and income status among American citizens. What he means by 'equality' in the economic context is simply the expectation on all sides that tomorrow 'I' can be as rich as 'you', or, conversely, that you can be as poor as I am today. The responsibility for both lies in the vagaries of commercial life, which make it the primary goal of the economic citizen to use them and influence them to his own advantage.

---

qualified to deal with foreign policy. Cf. DiA, 1.207, 209, 216, 243. This judgement on the mediocre and sinister political elites in the USA would later be repeated by Weber in many sarcastic remarks.

[57] DiA, 2.101. Cf. 1.271: 'I am not so much alarmed at the excessive liberty which reigns in that country as at the inadequate securities which one finds there against tyranny.'

The point here is that no one can be expected, and no one can be ordered, to be satisfied with less than any fellow citizen has. Prosperity is contingent, people are always upwardly as well as downwardly mobile, and there is no constant process of class-formation to be anticipated between those favoured by secure wealth, on the one hand, and the inescapably poor, on the other. This is the starting condition of 'equality', which explains a whole series of formative motivational processes.

The more the convergence of rich and poor has already taken place, the more powerful is everyone's ambition to overcome the last remaining difference and to catch up with, and possibly overtake, their better-off neighbours. Equality induces a desire for ever more equality, and even the smallest difference becomes the greatest annoyance. Democratic communities, observes Tocqueville in the United States, have a passion for equality which is 'ardent, insatiable, incessant, invincible; they call for equality in freedom; and if they cannot obtain that, they still call for equality in slavery.'[58] The motivations of phenomenal activity thus become dominant, stirred up by individualistic economic interests and an anxious striving for success always driven by fear of failure in business. The picture Tocqueville paints here is one of micro-tyranny, which economic citizens impose on themselves and one another – not unlike what Weber later called ascetic vocational life.

The dangers resulting from this micro-tyranny are the greater because majority rule applies not only in legislation and (because officials are elected) to the courts and the administrative system, but also in cultural life and opinion and will-formation among the people. The egalitarian-majoritarian loss of liberty occurs imperceptibly – and is therefore that much more disastrous. There is a brilliant formulation, which reappears more than a hundred years later as (the only) reference to Tocqueville in *Dialectic of Enlightenment*:[59] 'Monarchs . . . had materialized oppression;

---

[58] DiA, 2.102.

[59] Horkheimer and Adorno 1986, 133; Lassman calls this Tocqueville quote 'Tocqueville's version of [the] Dialectic of Enlightenment' (1993, 108).

the democratic republics of the present day have rendered it entirely an affair of the mind . . .. Under the absolute sway of one man the body was attacked in order to subdue the soul . . .. Such is not the course adopted by tyranny in democratic republics; there the body is left free, and the soul is enslaved.'[60] The point is clear: whereas the body reacts to a blow with pain, the soul is anaesthetized and rendered completely defenceless when it is taken under external control.

A drawback of commercial activity based on possessive individualism is the monotony of life, the melancholy and 'strange unrest'[61] of business people, who cannot enjoy what they have earned,[62] and the loss of republican virtues. 'In their intense and exclusive anxiety to make a fortune they lose sight of the close connection that exists between the private fortune of each and the prosperity of all. It is not necessary to do violence to such a people in order to strip them of the rights they enjoy; they themselves willingly loosen their hold.'[63] The exercise of their political rights becomes an annoying disruption that keeps them from their business. '[T]he better to look after what they call their own business, they neglect their chief business, which is to remain their own masters.'[64] The relentless driving power of an egalitarian commercial society produces *de*forming effects, so to speak endogenous injuries of socialization, and steers citizens towards a political self-expropriation, a tyranny not only over dissenting opinion and cultural minorities but also over themselves. The atrophy of political competence and judgement in

---

[60] DiA, 1.274. It is no longer the case that the authorities punish 'the body of the thought', which results in the escalation of political conflict, but rather that they seize hold of the substance of thought – resulting in conformist acquiescence.

[61] DiA, 2.145.

[62] Cf. Weber's well-known angry verdict against the mental deformations rampant in advanced capitalist society: 'Specialists without spirit, sensualists without heart; this nullity imagines that it has attained a level of civilization never before achieved' (Weber 1958b, 182).

[63] DiA, 2.149.

[64] Ibid.

public affairs, anti-political tendencies and 'the *general apathy* which is the consequence of individualism',[65] a solitary view of life, an abandonment of public responsibility – these are the deformations for which Tocqueville blames the individualism of economic society that has turned into an undifferentiated conformity.[66] One and (as we shall see) *only* one of the consequences is the appropriation of the citizens' relinquished political powers by an increasingly centralized state power,[67] against which the individual citizen is completely defenceless. The individual economic citizen is indifferent in both the temporal dimension (he thinks neither of his ancestors nor of the well-being of his children) and the social dimension (contemporaries are 'as strangers to each other'). Democracy 'throws him forever upon himself alone and threatens in the end to confine him entirely within the solitude of his own heart.'[68]

Tocqueville cannot accept that, according to the principle of majority rule, not the 'best' but the 'most' become masters of the law – and that 'the theory of equality is thus applied to the intellects of men.'[69] We can understand him to mean that equality and the striving for ever more equality are reasonably safe as long as they are confined to economic competition (or to equality of the sexes, of which he approves).[70] Equality in the spheres of politics and culture, however, means that the majority's standards, principles and criteria of judgement will from now on apply to everyone – and this is where the danger to liberty begins. An electoral majority

[65] Appendix BB (to II 339), II 388.
[66] Cf. Wolin 2001, 352: 'The paradox of individualism is that, while seeming to favor individual differences and a cult of variety, it is, in actuality, a social creation, a product of the difference-denying cult of equality.'
[67] Cf. DiA, 2, book 4.
[68] DiA, 2.106. In the 1950s, many sociological diagnoses of the age in the USA, following Tocqueville, elaborated this connection between individualism, mass society and the dangers of centralized despotism. See Riesman 1953 and Kornhauser 1959.
[69] DiA, 1.265.
[70] DiA, 2, book 3, chaps. VIII–XII.

translates the prevailing preferences of the masses into laws; this makes them short-sighted, capricious and erratic, but at the same time irresistible,[71] because, when there is a structural minority, they 'can never hope to draw the majority over to their side'.[72] 'This state of things is harmful in itself and dangerous for the future.'[73] What deeply troubles the author about the 'democratic age' is the limited and unreliable link between egalitarian majority rule and the rule of law, together with the potential for tyranny and the arbitrary destruction of freedom that follow from this.[74]

We can follow Tocqueville's train of thought by distinguishing between two processes that he carefully observed. On the one hand, the idea of equality and the commercial calculation bound up with it take hold of spheres of life in which they have no legitimate place: politics, culture and the sphere of opinions. This idea leads Tocqueville to a clearly elaborated outline of a theory of mass culture or 'culture industry'. On the other hand, as Tocqueville perceives with remarkable insight, the egalitarian premisses of the citizens' occupational life wither in precisely the sphere that most affects them – in economic life. The latter point appears in the astonishing chapter of the second volume where (probably on the basis of views he formed in Britain, in Manchester)[75] he reflects on the rise of big capital and the end of egalitarian competitive capitalism, which bring with them a new kind of class-formation in democracy. He thus anticipates not only the theory of the culture industry but also the concentration of capital, conceived as a self-subversion of economic equality.

Let us look first at the latter complex of economic transformations: Tocqueville sees that egalitarian market relations among competing businessmen in America have led to an enormous increase in prosperity. He foresees a further

[71] DiA, 1.264–5.
[72] DiA, 1.266.
[73] Ibid.
[74] DiA, 1.269ff.
[75] See Wolin 2001, chap. 17, 346ff.

increase resulting from industrial production methods, larger firms, a high demand for capital, and an intensified division of labour. He is familiar with the works of Adam Smith, from which he has learned that, in the division of labour in large enterprises, the worker pays for his improved productivity with a decreased 'faculty of applying his mind to the direction of work':[76] 'it may be said . . . that in proportion as the workman improves, the man is degraded.'[77] 'The art advances, the artisan recedes.'[78] At the same time, 'wealthy and educated men come forward', a 'class of masters'.[79] 'The master and the workman have then here no similarity, and their differences increase every day.' Tocqueville asks: 'What is this but aristocracy?' – in his terminology the opposite of equality, the result of its self-destruction.[80] But he points out that this new 'aristocracy' differs from its pre-democratic predecessors in that its privileges are determined not by tradition and the legal system but by superior economic power; and so the new class of industrial 'masters' also is relieved of the social duties of the 'old' aristocracy. The employer, member of a new 'manufacturing aristocracy which is growing up under our eyes',[81] is concerned not with *particular* workers, or concrete persons, but simply with *anonymous* ('abstract', as Marx later put it) *labour power*. Nor do employers have any interest in 'governing' workers; they want only to 'use' them.[82]

Tocqueville's only other excursion into questions of political economy in the America book (after all, eight years before the *Communist Manifesto*!) is in the seventh chapter of the third part of the second volume. Here he deals with 'The Influence of Democracy on Wages'.[83] He refers to the

[76] DiA, 2.168.
[77] Ibid.
[78] DiA, 2.169.
[79] Ibid.
[80] Ibid.
[81] DiA, 2.171.
[82] Ibid.
[83] DiA, 2.199ff.

'great and gloomy exception' which breaks the rule that democracy *uniformly* raises prosperity. In the 'great industries', workers – and this too is a deforming effect of institutions – 'contract habits of body [!] and mind which unfit them for any other sort of toil.'[84] '[T]heir only property is in their hands.' '[T]hey stand, therefore, almost at the mercy of the master', particularly as 'he can reduce the wages of his workmen almost at pleasure and make from them what he loses by the chances of business.' Tocqueville concludes this section with the remark that 'This state of dependence and wretchedness . . . is [the most] deserving of the attention of the legislator.'[85]

As equality, always understood here as equal chances of market success and as the levelling of differences, has so to speak strayed outside *economic* life and will continue to do so for the foreseeable future, it intrudes into cultural life, which is increasingly governed by the pressures of conformity. This is the other deformation observed by the author. '[T]he civilization of our age has perfected despotism itself.'[86] In the age of equality the 'readiness to believe the multitude increases and opinion is more than ever mistress of the world.'[87] Not only in theoretical knowledge but also in aesthetic production Americans lack any original and significant contribution. He explains this non-event as a 'natural and inevitable result of equality' and its trivializing effects on science and art.[88] But in America, specific conditions such as the greed and covetousness learned in business life constantly divert the human mind from the pleasures of the imagination and from intellectual work, if they do not immediately contribute to the pursuit of wealth. Nevertheless, in a noteworthy challenge to his own argument, Tocqueville considers the possibility that, as in the Maslow scale of human motivation and John Stuart Mill's

---

[84] DiA, 2.200.
[85] DiA, 2.200–1, also 327.
[86] DiA, 1.274.
[87] DiA, 2.11.
[88] DiA, 2.36.

hierarchy of 'lower' vs. 'higher' desires,[89] once the require-ments of prosperity have been satisfied, 'the number of those who cultivate the sciences, letters, and the arts, becomes immense.'[90]

In the meantime, it seems to him that 'the taste for the useful predominates over the love of the beautiful in the heart of man.'[91] The individual artist on the supply side of the culture market also thinks this way, beginning to produce his work only on the criteria of marketability and profitabil-ity, in other words, with a view to low production costs and a high sale price. The artist is therefore guided by consumer preferences;[92] he can then reduce his unit costs either by mass production or by lowering quality. Aesthetic standards change from the 'great' to the pleasant and pretty. But, in order not to lose customers, the lowering of quality must be hidden and not easily detectable. This drives the art producer to dishonesty, even to counterfeit, in his use of materials: the Doric column of a dwelling that looks as if it has been carved out of marble consists instead of painted wood. The artist and the craftsman serve, and at the same time create, a demand for false luxury and a superficial differentiation of taste.

Similar practices occur in the field of literary production. There are many works, but few are produced by well-known authors, and their works are mainly imported from England. The United States still has no literature of its own.[93] American authors are mainly journalists and 'idea-mongers'.[94] They write for a reading public lacking literary education, which 'asks for beauties self-proffered and easily enjoyed'.[95] Aesthetic life in the USA prefers, to use Kant's words, 'pleasant' to 'beautiful' arts,[96] naturalism to idealism, and in

[89] Mill 1974.
[90] DiA, 2.41.
[91] DiA, 2.50.
[92] DiA, 2.51.
[93] DiA, 2.59.
[94] DiA, 2.64.
[95] DiA, 2.62.
[96] Kant 1952.

painting *likeness* (*Abbild*) to *imaginative model* (*Vorbild*). Democracy 'introduces the trading spirit into literature'.[97]

The same applies to culture in general. Tocqueville maintains that in the United States there are 'very few writers of distinction . . ., no great historians and not a single eminent poet'.[98] He does not, however, simply register this as a defect but shows yet again with an undertone of envy that he is impressed by the lack of (always contentious) 'general ideas' and their proponents in American intellectual life.[99] In politics, Americans 'furnish examples rather than lessons to the world'.[100] Tocqueville describes the aesthetic practices of democratic society with such sharp analytic insight that it raises the intriguing question of how far the theory of the culture industry developed (*mutatis mutandis*) a century later in *Dialectic of Enlightenment* actually went beyond him. At the same time, he strives in an exemplary way to set aside prejudice and lets his cultural aristocratic preferences show through only in passing, when he urges Americans to study Greek and Latin literature at elite universities.[101]

I have discussed some of the important points at which Alexis de Tocqueville analyses American society with an eye to Europe, always accompanying his analysis with a subtext about the defects and strengths of France and

[97] DiA, 2.64.

[98] DiA, 1.326.

[99] Cf. the concept of 'self-evidence' in the American Declaration of Independence. The notion of self-evidence makes it unnecessary to give reasons for the basic principles of the political community. They are so obvious to *all* human beings that giving reasons becomes even more harmful than useful. This is sometimes aphoristically expressed in the 'mentally economizing' maxim: 'The more reasons given, the more reasons to object'. The formula of self-evidence spares the need not only for reasons but also for a 'critical' determination of the limits of their application, and establishes the intellectual preconditions for a missionary, crusading self-consciousness, and finally for today's (paradoxical) 'unilateral universalism'. Anyone who does not accept this assertion of self-evidence must be either intellectually incompetent or morally deficient – and hence 'evil'.

[100] DiA, 1.326.

[101] DiA, 1, chap. 15.

Europe, and above all the foreseeable challenges they face. Of course, I can here touch upon far less than half the themes that Tocqueville deals with in his wide-ranging sociology of democracy, or, more precisely, his sociology of a society based on civil equality. Missing here are the theological themes, the sociology of religion, constitutional law, the sociology of the family and gender, the sociology of education and the court system, the extensive military sociology, and also those parts of the America book that deal in detail with sections of the population who did not *come* to America *of their own free will*, that is, (a) the indigenous inhabitants who did not 'come' at all (because they were always, in historical time, already there) and (b) those who came involuntarily – the slaves carried from Africa and their descendants. All these things would be important in any reasonably exhaustive account of a work whose author has not implausibly been judged the most significant political theorist of the nineteenth century.[102]

I would not want to end my very fragmentary survey of Tocqueville's America book without touching on the 'good' news presented by the author after he has investigated the freedom-destroying, tyrannical, conformist and despotic potential of 'equality', that is, of a society based on contractual market relations and competitive individualism, with its material insatiability. What countervailing forces are there to oppose the despotic potential of this new type of society and to ensure 'the maintenance of the democratic republic in the United States',[103] which, despite all his doubts, the author remains convinced will survive?

Three categories of 'favourable circumstances'[104] (the main theoretical variables of the work)[105] sustain Tocqueville's confidence: (1) contingent external conditions that are not

---

[102] Elster 1993, 101.

[103] DiA, 1.298.

[104] DiA, 1.300.

[105] Tocqueville postulates that customs are more decisive than institutions and laws, and the latter more important than natural 'conditions' (DiA, 1.330).

man-made, (2) laws and institutions, and (3) habits and customs.

On the first point, an economic and military-geographic argument comes into play, which the author emphasizes elsewhere too: the Americans have no equal neighbours and therefore need fear neither *war nor conquest*, nor, for that reason, the domestic power of a military caste. In addition, they possess an empty, large and rich country and therefore (also because of the currents of migration this permits) need not fear *hardship or poverty*; nor need they fear despotism, because a large country must be decentralized and avoids the dangers of centralization just by its geographic nature. 'General prosperity is favourable to the stability of all governments.'[106] Neither the ambition of a leader nor the hardship of the people can therefore become a source of instability. The 'unbounded desire of riches'[107] does not drive the people, in their 'restless disposition', to gather together in one place to make threatening demands; it leads them instead to conflict-free 'exit'-reactions in a positive-sum game, that is, to the dispersal and dilution of the greedy in 'empty' spaces instead of the concentration of political passions in large cities.[108]

Second, there are American laws and institutions that encourage stability and prevent tyranny. Throughout his work,[109] Tocqueville – in this respect as in others a predecessor of Max Weber – regards bureaucratic centralism as a gateway to, and a manifestation of, tyranny and the loss of liberty. Therefore, his confident predictions about the stability of the republic are based on the distinctive vertical division of powers (among the federal government, the states and autonomous municipalities) as well as on the horizontal division of powers, above all the independence of the courts. It is not primarily the rule of law but the fact that American judges have the power to make law by

---

[106] DiA, 1.301.
[107] DiA, 1.306.
[108] Cf. Sombart 1976.
[109] See Tocqueville 1951.

interpreting the Constitution that Tocqueville (a judge himself!) regards as a guarantee that the courts will 'check and direct the impulses of the majority without stopping its activity',[110] serve as 'powerful barriers . . . against tyranny'[111] and constitute 'the most powerful, if not the only, counterpoise to the democratic element'.[112] Tocqueville regards it as one of the benefits of trial by jury that it educates the people at the same time: as a free 'public school, ever open', the courts impart to all citizens something of the judge's 'habits of thought'.[113]

The third, most important variable in explaining the expected stability of the republic and its immunity from the dangers of tyranny lies in customs – i.e. 'habits of the heart' as well as the 'character of mind', that is, 'the whole moral and intellectual condition of a people'.[114] This condition is determined partly by Christian religion, which can act as a unifying and socially integrative counterweight against the dangers of tyranny precisely because of the strict separation of church and state. The beneficial political effect of Christianity rests, for Tocqueville, largely on the fact that in the United States it is not politicized; religion, because of the prudent self-limitation of the clergy, is detached from political conflict. Religious communities retain 'power over the soul' precisely *because* they have renounced political power. They do not, however, simply withdraw from political life but rather, by means of their formative function, that is, through the self-organization of communal life in sects and churches, indirectly help Americans to practise the 'art of being free'.[115] The author is convinced that the Christian doctrine of salvation and the prospect of life after death can extend the time horizons shortened by individualism and accustom people to prefer their long-term 'self-interest rightly understood', as it

[110] DiA, 1.310.
[111] DiA, 1.107.
[112] DiA, 1.288.
[113] DiA, 1.296–7.
[114] DiA, 1.310. See also 326–42.
[115] DiA, 1.314.

were their *stakeholder* interests instead of their momentary *shareholder* interests.[116]

In addition, American 'customs' find expression in the associative relations of civic organizations. One may regard these organizations, as Max Weber later did, as a secularized and purposive-rational version of religious sects. Tocqueville's thesis is that 'the Americans combat the effects of individualism by free institutions',[117] that is, precisely such organizations in civil society; this organizational life is, in his eyes, the most important counterweight to the despotic and dependence-generating tendencies of individualism and mass society.[118] With his characteristic mixture of aristocratic values and sensitivity to civil society, he formulates a jewel of social-scientific insight: 'A despot easily forgives his subjects for not loving him, provided they do not love each other.'[119] He observes that Americans 'constantly form associations',[120] and that they do so in fulfilment, so to speak, of the anti-individualistic duty 'to make themselves useful to their fellow creatures',[121] understanding that collective self-help serves their own interests:[122] to 'give entertainments, to found seminaries, to build inns, to construct churches, to diffuse books, to send missionaries to the antipodes . . . [and to] found hospitals, prisons, and schools'.[123] Both duty and

---

[116] DiA, 2.129–35.

[117] This is the title of chap. 4, book 2, of vol. 2, 109ff.

[118] There is also in Tocqueville a welfare state critique *avant la lettre* (e.g. DiA, 1.93–4), though not from a market-liberal point of view but rather from the perspective of a political liberalism grounded in civil society.

[119] DiA, 2.109. This insight suggests itself for the analysis of 'totalitarian' and also post-authoritarian societies. Cf. Howard 2003.

[120] DiA, 2.114.

[121] DiA, 2.112.

[122] Because there is no preventive police supervision in the United States, such as fire-prevention rules regulating the construction of buildings, 'fires are more frequent than in Europe; but, in general, they are more speedily extinguished, because the surrounding population is prompt to lend assistance' (Appendix I (to vol. 1. 98), 2.371).

[123] DiA, 2.114. The examples primarily concern, and are confined to, association for religious and cultural projects, as well as for communal

interest are at first 'intentional' but then become 'instinct' or a collective and habitually practised 'art' of association.[124] People join together not on the basis of law and custom but because of 'the accidental similarity of opinion and tastes; hence private society is infinitely varied.'[125]

Tocqueville likes to discuss the American temperance unions, devoted to the struggle against drunkenness. It seemed to him at first 'more like a joke' that 'a hundred thousand men had bound themselves publicly to abstain from spirituous liquor.' Why could they not 'content themselves with drinking water by their own firesides?' But, in comparison to France, he sees the value of this missionary self-education in civil society. 'It is probable that if these hundred thousand men had lived in France, each of them would singly have petitioned the government to control the public houses all over the kingdom.'[126]

Three conclusions can be drawn, with implications for the diagnosis of Europe's present and future, from Tocqueville's contemporary perspective:

1 Europe and America have both participated in the world-historic trend toward 'equality', that is, the erosion of status privilege structures, which Tocqueville sees at work in Europe since the eleventh century. The spatial distance between Europe and America is at the same time a world-historic distance. The United States is a positive avant-garde. It has already reached the 'democratic age' that is the constant theme of the second volume of *Democracy in*

infrastructure. In that respect, there is a contrast, but perhaps also a relation of influence, with the concept of association that Marx (and later Gramsci) constantly uses in describing the relations of post-capitalist society. Cf. Marx and Engels 1959–, vol. 25. 267, 456, 828. There is a very direct connection between Tocqueville's 'art' of association and the concept of 'social capital', which, since Putnam's book (1993), has been the subject of much social science research in the United States and internationally.

124 DiA, 2.112, 115.
125 DiA, 2.227.
126 DiA, 2.118. Translation modified.

America. In Europe the transition is yet to come, admittedly under essentially unfavourable conditions, because Europe must first overcome and abolish a political power[127] obsessed with control and centralization, a power which, fortunately for Americans, has never existed on their side of the Atlantic.

2 'Democracy', the political and above all social characteristic of the coming age, is a thoroughly precarious institutional arrangement threatened less with a lapse into anarchy than with despotism. Whether the democratic regime is stable depends on favourable conditions not subject to human control. In America, a large and rich country constituting a *tabula rasa* on which to build a new society, the breakthrough to equal freedom and durable democracy was significantly easier to achieve than it could ever be in Europe. In Europe, equality presupposes a revolution at least in consciousness and customs, and therefore the *political education* and *ideological mobilization* of citizens, which often enough lead to a new despotism. By contrast, liberty and equality in America have been achieved spontaneously and, as it were, unreflexively, by means of formative and partly, to be sure, also *de*forming effects, which the citizens have absorbed through non-theoretical habituation.[128]

3 Because of its historical burdens, Europe finds itself in the position of a latecomer in relation to American development. Tocqueville emphasizes the American social model's extraordinary power of expansion and hazards a prognosis that must have seemed almost mad at a time (1834) when the population of the United States was 13 million (in the then only twenty-two states): that the population will one day reach 150 million, 'all belonging to one family, owing

---

127 See DiA, 2, part 4, chap. 5, 314ff.
128 The theory-free nature of American customs and habits of life, the preference for 'good sense' and 'positive calculations' as against speculation, is a central theme of Tocqueville's portrait of America, to which he constantly returns. See DiA, 1.308.

their origin to the same cause, and preserving the same civilization, the same language, the same religion, the same habits, the same manners, and imbued with the same opinions, propagated under the same forms.'[129] Europe has nothing to match this 'fact new to the world'.[130] He concludes the first volume of his America book, published in 1835, with the prediction that *Russia* is far more likely to form a counterweight. America and Russia seem to him 'marked out by the will of Heaven to sway the destinies of half the globe'.[131] Americans struggle successfully with nature and rely on 'the unguided strength and common sense of the people', while 'the adversaries of the Russian are men' and 'all the authority in society [is centred] in a single arm.'[132] Tocqueville can see no role for Europe in this astonishingly visionary scenario.

Excursus on Rules and Decisions

A pillar of Tocqueville's theory of the 'democratic age', based on the American example, is the thesis that democracies are stable when and because they have religious and secular associational structures and means of community formation that are able to counter the two pathologies of 'equality': individualism and despotism. Looking back today at this most famous of Tocqueville's hypotheses, three kinds of doubts arise about its continuing validity. One question concerns the robustness of associational practices that emerged out of the settlers' sectarian life and were inspired by its spirit. These are the practices to which American society in its own self-description, both in everyday life and in the social sciences, applies the concept of *community* (a concept which, in its social semantic, cannot adequately be translated into

---

[129] DiA, 1.451–2.
[130] Ibid.
[131] Ibid.
[132] Ibid.

German).[133] This refers to a kind of 'community formation' that is local and 'voluntaristic' (i.e. based on voluntary membership and interaction among those physically present), but which is at the same time free of tribal or ethnic presuppositions, and also free of formal authority relations, whether internal or external.[134] Since the 1960s, there has existed in the United States itself a wide current of social science literature which, from a more or less nostalgic perspective, both diagnoses and laments the decline of these associational 'habits of the heart' and the Tocquevillean 'art of association'.[135] A second strand of discussion – as we shall see in Max Weber's treatment of this theme – concerns the 'disenchantment' of American associational life, that is, its mobilization for purposes of social control, pressures for conformity or economic interests in the formation of cartels and exclusive, neo-feudal hierarchies. There is also a third sceptical argument, namely, that the religiously based micro-republicanism of local communities (even where it remains unadulterated) conditions a specifically American form of state authority which, from a European point of view, is deviant and deficient, that is, structurally blocked and distorted by communitarian localism. To the extent that this is a valid objection, Tocqueville's 'civil society' solutions to the problems of individualism and despotism would have to be dismissed as illusory even if they were still practicable in the current conditions of American society.

It is well known that the legal and constitutional foundation of the 'separation of church and state' can be directed towards two diametrically opposed conceptions of social and legal order.[136] In Europe, it has a secularizing function, modifying the territorial system of religion introduced in 1648 by the Treaty of Westphalia and thereby suppressing the *influence of religion on national politics*. In the USA, whose

[133] Joas 1993.
[134] Galston 2000, 64ff.
[135] A current example of this literature is Putnam 2000: 'For American sociology . . . the perspective of loss of community is absolutely constitutive.' Cf. Joas 1993.
[136] On the following, see Haller 2002.

historical foundation and modern self-image are bound up with the fate of European religious refugees, the separation of church and state means *protecting religion from state power* and ensuring its free development in the framework of voluntary religious communities, the opposite of European state churches. The defining principle of the American case, therefore, is not mistrust of the church's influence on public life but rather mistrust of state power, which is regarded with suspicion because of its tendency to restrict, regulate or bestow selective privileges on religious communities and all other associations in civil society which in part have emerged out of such communities.[137]

State power in the USA is, both normatively and in the institutional structure of government, limited to the mandate of protecting the citizen from the state (and, *a fortiori*, from the harmful effects of actions by foreign states and non-state actors). On the other hand, it is restricted in its ability to protect the liberty of citizens from other threats originating in societal actors and the damage they can inflict on one another's liberties.[138] When citizens want to defend

---

[137] Cf. the *establishment clause* in the First Amendment of the US Constitution.

[138] This doctrine, which has at the same time acted as a barrier to the development of the USA into a welfare state on the European model, has often been strengthened by the Supreme Court, as in the ruling that the essence of the Constitution is 'to protect the people from the State, not to ensure that the State protect[s] them from each other . . . [due process is a] limitation on the State's power to act, not . . . a guarantee of certain minimum levels of safety and security' (San Antonio Independent School District v. Rodriguez, 411 U.S. 1, 59 [1973]). Similar is the ruling that 'the Constitution is a charter of negative rather than positive liberties . . . .. The men who wrote the Bill of Rights were not concerned that government might do too little for the people but that it might do too much to them . . . .. the difference between harming and failing to help is just the difference . . . between negative liberty – being let alone by the state – and positive liberty – being helped by it' (Jackson v. City of Joliet, 715 F2D [1983]). See Abraham 1996 for an analysis of this self-limitation of the state which is based not on economic liberalism alone but also on constitutional theory.

themselves against *this* kind of damage, they must do it as individuals *in court* and obtain a *decision*; they cannot do it by virtue of participation in some kind of collective popular sovereignty *through legislation* and legally established *rules*. The suspicion of any social service provided by the state is nourished by the constitutional order and is constantly renewed in its virulence; and it means that, from the beginning and still today, political elites have felt obliged to represent the identity of the American nation as a community of free religious communities in 'God's own country', by means of official symbols ('God bless America', 'In God we trust', 'City on the Hill') and gestures of deference towards the religious life (the President shows himself in public, with his family, leaving a place of worship after church on Sunday). Both the citizens' mistrust of the state and the zealously God-fearing appeasement of that mistrust by the elites have a secular counterpart in the federal separation of powers established by the Constitution, which limits the powers of the central state, and also in the unreflexive preference which the majority of American citizens have for 'less tax' instead of 'more state services' – particularly since an increase in, for instance, social and cultural state services might hinder the activities and charitable services of voluntary religious communities, as well as those of educational and cultural private foundations. The ideal of a society emancipated from state power therefore has, far beyond any property interests and market liberalism, a religious kernel in the idea that divine laws (in a plurality of interpretations) take precedence over legal rules laid down by a popular sovereign. The integration of society is not, as in Europe, the work of a state power imposing social order but rather of religious communities and, for all their denominational and sectarian fragmentation, their common orientation towards religious salvation.

The integration of American society rests on a unique configuration of *nation-building* without prior *state-building*. The precedence of society over state can be explained historically by the conditions of the first settler communities, which escaped European state powers and their religious systems, and the constant push of migrants over the *frontier*, pressing into territories where no state power yet existed. This 'horizontal' mode[139] of forming a political community is voluntary and rests on the belief, consent and commitment of citizens uniting in manifold associations, not on supervision and legal compulsion exercised by a state power. In the United States *court decisions* or civil law *contract* assume the role played in Europe by legislatures and by political struggles over the content of laws having to do with society's power over itself,[140] mediated by *legislation*. In the American case, individual and group interests can be brought to bear and balanced out against each other, without having to fall back on a notional 'popular sovereignty' present in parliament, like the one arising from European constitutional thought, which in the USA is regarded as fraught with risks. This procedurally regulated but substantively 'sub-legal' balancing of interests through the courts and lawyers rests on ad hoc *decisions* in a field of relatively limited legal rules. Other factors come into play in affecting these decisions: the exercise of influence and power resources, locally adhered-to moral principles and also economic resources which the adversaries bring to the legal battle and to which its outcome is open. This is so precisely because such decisions are at best weakly determined by substantive statutory *rules*, which in a universalistic and at the same time calculable manner resolve conflicts of interest by means of a legislatively considered and deliberate balance. In the manner of Tocqueville's daring generalizations, we might say that, in America, the law books are thin, but for that very reason the contractual agreements worked out by means of civil law are proportionally more voluminous.

The emancipation of society from the habitually mistrusted state power is also served by the horizontal division of power, as well as the vertical fragmentation of state power through a wide-ranging system of fiscal and legislative autonomy for local authorities and individual state governments in the

---

[139] Cf. Preuss 1994 and Preuss 1990, 23ff.
[140] See Heller 1934.

American form of federalism. This produces a maximum of constitutionally established veto points against the federal government (quite apart from the *de facto* veto power exercised by capital and organized interests, as they operate, for example, through the system of electoral finance). The exception to this many-sided fragmentation of state power is, above all, the competence of Congress, as the federal legislative body, to legislate on the indispensable requirements of a capitalist economy – such as monetary and defence policy, federal taxes, commercial and bankruptcy law, social security and the immigration regime. Beyond that, the autonomy of the constituent territorial units is limited by federal prerogative almost only in those policy areas that have to do with the protection, through security and commercial policy, of national interests against *external* opponents and rivals. In order to assert its powers, to extract the necessary financial means in a relatively conflict-free way, and, in general, to protect its sphere of activity, the federal government, especially the presidency as the central power in external economic and political matters, needs security-related justifications in the form of 'enemies' and the (military, ideological, economic) threats and dangers ascribed to them. Characteristically derived from such security concerns are federal regulations and programmes which in any other country would be considered purely 'domestic' matters – such as vocational training (the 'National Defense Education Act' enacted after the Sputnik shock in 1957), promotion of scientific research, a system of public hospitals ('veterans' hospitals'), or long-distance road construction ('Interstate and Defense Highway System'). Where there are no security concerns to lend support – as in the still unresolved problem of a public health insurance system covering the whole population – federal legislative initiatives are blocked (as in the first Clinton administration and its failed health reform) at the constitutional and *de facto* veto points.

The 'associative' defence mechanisms, supposedly directed against both the hypertrophy of individualism and the dangers of despotism, have produced in the United States – and here is the 'bad' news from a European point of view, to be set against the 'good' laid out by Tocqueville – a central state power so enfeebled in domestic politics that, driven by corporate interests, its primary sphere of activity lies in economic and security-related areas of foreign policy. Supported by the certainty of 'self-evident' political and moral criteria for distinguishing 'good' from 'evil', the federal state asserts itself by means of expansionist ventures for control of the international environment. Tocqueville welcomed everything that seemed to him a check on atomistic economic individualism and on the concentration of central state power, above all the local associational and sectarian life of Americans. He did not and could not yet see[141] that an excessively limited state power might one day be unable to carry out its indispensable function of integrating a complex society, and that for this reason, on structural grounds, in a constant search for opportunities to confirm or apply its precarious ability to act, it would seek to compensate for the deficit in its *internal* governing capacity by taking control of the outside world and integrating society through the legitimation provided by *external* enemies and dangers. Because in American constitutional thought there is no national 'popular sovereignty' that could determine domestic conditions by legislative means, there is a much more sharply accentuated 'state sovereignty', which asserts itself – whether in isolationist or interventionist ways – in the external relations of the USA. The authors of the *Federalist Papers*, the foundational document of American federal power, already justified the necessity of that power on the grounds of 'dangers from foreign force' and 'the utility of the union in respect to commercial relations and a navy'.[142] At least one school of international relations theory, the 'realist' school, is dominated by the affirmative self-description (and self-admiration) of

---

[141] Cf., however, Tocqueville's clear-sighted reflection on 'the happiest consequences of the absence of government (when a people is fortunate enough to be able to do without it, which is rare)' (quoted from Jardin 1988, 152).

[142] *Federalist Papers* no. 2 and no. 11.

the United States as a model for the rest of the world, as a missionary power that must help to spread its own values throughout the world, adopting the methods of a modern crusade, and endeavours to secure its successes by imperial domination.[143] These efforts express the longing to transcend boundaries, moving ever further towards the shifting 'frontier' celebrated in the heroic narrative of American history, so that, then as now, 'the constant shifting of the border . . . is prophetically, not just economically, motivated'.[144] As current developments since 11 September 2001 have illustrated, in all these projects this dominant power proceeds, in its (now for the first time structurally unendable) war against 'evil' and for 'good', not by rule-bound but by decision-bound principles, not in the framework of recognized international law and human rights norms but unilaterally, even if supported at the time by an alleged 'coalition of the willing' of individual states. This policy of voluntaristic coalition-building may be understood as precisely a resurrection of the spirit of voluntary sects and local associations on the plane of international politics.

Foreign ventures by a federal executive that is impoverished in respect of its domestic policy-making capacity serve not only to compensate for its own limitations but also, internally, to consolidate the American nation as a distinctive community of values. As American values are carried throughout the world and opposed to 'evil', their precarious effectiveness inside the society is strengthened and forms the basis on which society as a whole, in spite of all its divisions, describes itself as a stronghold of the 'good'. This good consists, as Tocqueville's clear-sighted analysis shows, in a synthesis of possessive individualism and religious (or civil-religious republican) community. The knowledge of this good is of a religious kind, as he also clearly explained, not so much in its content as in its *form*. It rests, in a manner analogous to religious revelation and the certainty of salvation that flows

[143] Morgenthau 1978.
[144] Kamphausen 1991, 259.

from it, on a pre-reflexive 'epistemology of *self-evidence*',[145] on a groundless consciousness of revelation, not on rational grounds, as in political and legal contract theory. In this way, foreign policy, as it frees itself from the fetters of international law and strives to spread those 'self-evident' American values throughout the world, reinforces the idea that the nation in whose name this takes place is cooperating with Providence in its plan for salvation and thereby proving its place among the elect.

[145] See ibid., 264.

3
Max Weber: American Escape Routes from the Iron Cage?

It is obviously impossible here to present the whole content of Weber's diagnosis of contemporary society, or even to elaborate his 'problematic'.[1] Weber, as is well known, set himself the gigantic task of explaining 'the special peculiarity of Occidental rationalism, and within this field that of the modern Occidental form'.[2] It is not entirely clear here what, for Weber, is the spatial reach of the 'Occident' ('the West'): the alternatives that come to mind are Western Europe, Europe, Europe and North America, or even all of these plus the 'new countries'[3] of the modern world, that is, the postcolonial settler societies. Weber is not consistent as to which of these he has in mind when he speaks of 'the Occident'. In the essays on the sociology of knowledge he explains how the object under investigation is constituted, e.g. 'everything "modern", that is, our Christian-capitalist-constitutional culture, "radiating out" from Europe, in its current phase'.[4] In that respect, Europe appears as the dynamic core of the 'Occident'. Then he also speaks of

[1] See Hennis 2000a.
[2] PE, 26.
[3] ES, 890.
[4] GAWL, 257.

'our European-American social and economic life', which 'is "rationalized" in a specific way and in a specific sense', and stresses that 'explanation of this rationalization and . . . analysis of related phenomena is one of the chief tasks of our disciplines.'[5] In this version, then, 'rationalization' is treated as a transatlantic phenomenon. The scope is again narrowed when he speaks of 'Western European and American capitalism',[6] and further of the 'modern European Occident'.[7] Here, the kind and degree of inclusion of North America in the formation 'Occident' becomes uncertain again. This also applies when Weber writes about the convergence of the United States and Europe in the essay on 'Protestant Sects and the Spirit of Capitalism', composed immediately after his return from his American journey, which would later be repeatedly expanded, as well as in the second part of the Protestant Ethic, also written under the influence of his journey. In the barely thirty pages (in the 1920 version) of this text, Weber, speaking of certain phenomena in the sociology of religion, refers twice to the 'Europeanization' of American society.[8]

Weber thus takes the view that American society is beginning to fall in line with a structural type already present and dominant in Europe.[9] He sees the United States in the role of latecomer, an 'unfinished Europe'[10] (because, among other things, society has not yet fully grown into its territorial boundaries but is still in the process of conquering the territory of the state and its current 'new frontier'). The USA is still enjoying, though less and less so, the legacy of a

---

[5] 'The Meaning of Ethical Neutrality in Sociology and Economics', in Weber 1949, 34.
[6] PE, 52; emphasis added.
[7] GARS 1, 348; emphases added.
[8] Weber 1958c (hereafter 'Sects'), 302.
[9] Weber reaffirms this assessment ('Europeanization') in a lecture in March 1918 on the theme 'Democracy and Aristocracy in American Life', although the content of this lecture is known only through three press reports.
[10] Kamphausen 2002, 145.

happier past, but in the foreseeable future it will take the European path.[11]

My purpose here is to shed light on the systematic meaning that Weber's experience of American social conditions had for his work and for his perspective on Europe's present and future. Does America offer a different *and* robust alternative path, which diverges from the European model of industrial society and political modernization? Is American society acquiring an 'authentic difference'?[12] Or are there stronger indications that the United States is indeed being 'Europeanized' and will therefore, with a certain delay, partake in the developmental logic of 'the' model of occidental rationalism? Weber was confronted with an anomaly in the United States, which set him the problem of how to treat the observable realities that deviated from European, and particularly German, conditions: whether he should incorporate them into 'occidental' rationalism or consider, at least theoretically, that this divergent pattern in the process of Western modernization might represent a different path of development. As we shall see, Weber never reached a clear answer to this question, so important for his own theoretical work.

From 1904 until the late lecture on socialism (1918),[13] but above all in almost every major section of *Economy and Society*, Weber confronted the problem that certain social facts in the United States did not completely fit his deeply pessimistic theory of 'occidental rationalism'. We shall look at how he handles these provocative American anomalies in his social diagnosis.

[11] To support the 'Europeanization' hypothesis, Weber makes use of arguments that had already (in a rougher form) been elaborated by Werner Sombart (1906): the creation of a 'free land' beyond the *frontier* and the consequences of waves of immigration (Sombart 1906, 71) characterized as 'social panmixia'. As we shall see, Weber also considers the erosion of the egalitarian everyday culture grounded on the structures of voluntary associations. See also Weber 1952.

[12] Kamphausen 2002, 147, 163ff.

[13] 'Socialism', in SSP.

In his work on the sociology of law, economy, religion and politics, where he tries to impose a typological order on the infinite diversity of events and phenomena, Weber focuses on no other country except Germany with the same constant and intensive attention that he devotes to conditions in the United States.[14] Both the Munich lectures on 'Science as a Vocation' and 'Politics as a Vocation' also develop their arguments in relation, and in contrast, to American conditions. The same applies to the Weberian sociology of religion, particularly *The Protestant Ethic and the Spirit of Capitalism*, of which part 2[15] was written immediately after his stay in America.[16] I would argue that America stood at the centre of his research programme, because, despite all his reservations, it represented for him a 'picture of freedom'[17] to be held up as a warning against the weak, timid, depoliticized, opportunistic 'indifferentism' of Europeans.[18]

But first, let us look at the experiences and observations that Weber brought home from the thirteen weeks of his only visit to the USA, in the autumn of 1904.[19] Those weeks were characterized for Weber by an extreme intensity of observation, a wide variety of contacts and enormous effort in the collection of impressions and primary social-scientific data and sources. In this respect, he was far ahead of Ernst Troeltsch and Werner Sombart, who travelled with him to the same congress in St Louis.[20] In her biography of Weber,

---

[14] Wolfgang Mommsen's thesis that 'the United States never played a central role in Weber's thought' (Mommsen 1974b, 73) is simply incomprehensible and is deservedly attacked (Hecht 1998, 159; Kamphausen 2002, 183).

[15] 'The Practical Ethics of the Ascetic Branches of Protestantism', 95–183.

[16] Eisermann 1968, 22. But Weber had already conceived his thesis on the affinity between Protestant (actually Puritan) religiosity and the spirit of capitalism before his trip to America.

[17] Hecht 1998, 161.

[18] Ibid., 156–66.

[19] Marianne Weber 1975, 279–304. Cf. Rollmann 1993; Scaff 1998; Roth 2001, chap. 14.

[20] This was an international Congress of Arts and Sciences organized in connection with the World's Fair in St Louis.

Marianne Weber reports on the enthusiasm and intense observation with which, even while recovering from a depressive illness, he opened himself to encounters with a wide variety of people, places and institutional sectors. The main stops were New York, Buffalo, Niagara Falls, Chicago, St Louis, Washington, Oklahoma City, New Orleans, Philadelphia, Boston and again New York.[21] Marianne Weber, like Weber himself in the (still unpublished) letters he wrote about this journey, reports with great sympathy and often a trace of envious admiration the thrilling impressions made, for instance, by the 'audacious residential towers' of Manhattan; the stronghold of capital at the southern tip of the island; the 'citadels of the business world';[22] the 'exorbitant' kindness, friendliness and modesty of Americans in their contacts with foreigners and their courtesy and lack of affectation; the degenerate poverty of multi-ethnic Chicago, plagued with filth, violence and accidents; the practical-political ethos of socialist, reform-minded, feminist and social worker activists such as Jane Addams and the factory inspector Florence Kelly; observation of the life of the indigenous Indians; confrontation with sectarian fanaticism and the 'power of church communities'; racial division and the situation of the black population, which Weber later took up in correspondence with the two opposing leaders of the black community, Booker T. Washington and W. E. B. Du Bois;[23] the admirable academic-educational spirit of the Quaker colleges Bryn Mawr and Haverford; the academic patronage and sporting events at the universities; his meeting with William James at Harvard and with his own émigré relatives; the

---

[21] The choice of itinerary, apart from a commitment in Chicago, arose in part from a visit Weber paid to relatives who had emigrated (to Oklahoma City). Nevertheless, the similarity with the route taken by Tocqueville and Beaumont is worth noting.

[22] Marianne Weber 1975, 281, 283.

[23] William Edward Burghardt Du Bois (1868–1963), later the first black PhD at Harvard, had at the beginning of 1890 studied in Germany at the Friedrich-Wilhelm University, Berlin, as a scholarship student, where he also studied with the young lecturer Max Weber.

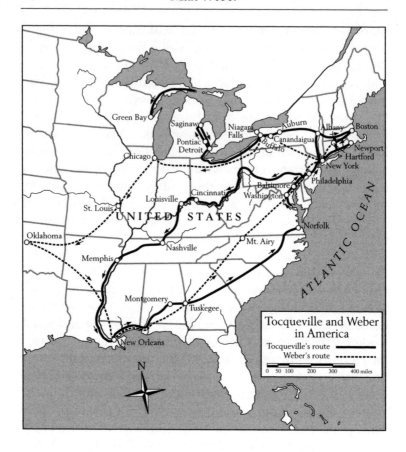

Tocqueville and Weber
in America
Tocqueville's route ——————
Weber's route ------------
0 50 100   200   300   400 miles

beginnings of the oil industry in the South; the social and
pedagogical institutions of New York's Jewish communities.
Weber himself experienced his almost obsessive immersion
in these sectors of American society as a 'remedy' that con-
tributed to the recovery of his health, and on his return
journey he wrote that 'the [scientific] fruits [of the journey]
can, of course, not be seen for some time.'[24]

---

[24] Marianne Weber 1975, 304. Werner Sombart, who travelled with him,
had a completely different attitude, sending 'warm greetings . . . from
this dreadful cultural hell' (quoted from Kaesler 2004).

Weber, I would argue, brought from America a social-theoretical theme for his life's work: namely, the question[25] of whether US society represented a viable social and political formation that might even be reproduced in Europe; whether this might make it at least possible to avoid the bureaucratization, rationalization, reification, depersonalization, secularization and meaningless occupational and professional specialization (*Berufs- und Fachmenschentum*) encouraged by capitalism; and whether individual freedom could thus be preserved not only (as he would later, resignedly, formulate it)[26] for small minorities[27] at the *top* of state, party and administrative apparatuses but collectively at the *base* of the citizen body and its associations.[28] His travelling companion Troeltsch reported Weber's 'enthusiasm for the new land' and his 'total admiration for its wonderful people'. 'His love in the fight and engagement for the individual finds here entire satisfaction.'[29] Weber was 'almost intoxicated by the dynamic of American work and industry, but also aware of the potential freedom for the creative individual.'[30] His enthusiastic admiration for conditions of life in the USA and the opportunities available there for a 'free way of life'[31] would, as we shall see, fade significantly on later consideration.

The question that motivated Weber's interest in the United States was whether an alternative and preferable model of capitalist modernization and liberal democracy was discernible there. Should the foreseeable process of development be conceived as America catching up with Europe – that is, Europeanization of America – or is it more

---

[25] See Scaff 1998, 77.
[26] 'The President of the Reich', in Weber 1994, 307.
[27] Weber never doubted the premise that policy is always made by minorities and important decisions always by a few. See Portinaro 2001, 288. He pronounced vigorously on the 'absolutely blind faith in the infallibility and omnipotence of the majority' (GPS, 488).
[28] See Scaff 1998, 63.
[29] Quoted from Rollmann 1993, 372.
[30] Rollmann 1993, 373.
[31] Kamphausen 2002, 186.

likely to be a liberating 'Americanization of Europe'? In
Weber's observations, the diagnosis of a Europeanization of
America clearly predominates – that is, the delayed but ultimately inexorable assimilation of American to European
societal conditions. Emigration to the USA, it seems, offers
no escape from the disasters of occidental rationalism.[32] Any
other conclusion would have undermined many of his conceptual and diagnostic premises, or would at least have
required them to be revised. The question must be raised as
to what extent Weber's efforts to reduce American excep-
tionalism to a transitional phenomenon[33] was motivated by
a kind of consistency pressure to make it conform to his own
theoretical constructions, which could tolerate no truly
lasting alternative model or exception. All the more does it
seem to me evidence of Weber's scientific ethos and his
honesty as a scholar that, when the convergence hypothesis
reappears in his later work, he subjects it to a series of self-
critical objections.

In what follows, I shall explore the arguments and observations with which Weber highlights the structural peculiar-
ities and deviations of American society, then seeks to dismiss
them as transitory and inessential, and finally (without resolv-
ing his own objections) subsumes the American case too
under the general formula of a human condition deformed,
here as well as there, by occidental rationalism.[34] For all his
initial enthusiasm and continuing sympathy for the exceptional conditions of a free way of life which he had encountered in the USA, his analysis gravitates towards a levelling of
differences, the expectation of a Europeanization of America
and an integral model of a single unified process of rationalization, bureaucratization and secularization, driven by the
mechanics of economic gain.[35]

---

[32] See Eisermann 1968, 11.
[33] Weber (like Sombart) thus expected that, with some delay, a workers'
   movement with a class party would also emerge in the United States.
   See Mommsen 1974b, 79.
[34] Kamphausen 2002, 195f.
[35] Ibid., 265ff.

Weber sees two evolutionary laws at work in the world of occidental rationalism. First, there is the advancing *expropriation* of human beings in all institutional spheres, an expropriation not only in the material sense of separation of the person from the material means of production[36] but also as the ' "soullessness" of following' and the followers' 'intellectual proletarianization',[37] as he sees them in the internal life of modern mass parties. As a consequence of this general tendency, people are robbed not only of their property but of responsibility for themselves and of the opportunity to exercise it. Second, 'specialists without spirit, sensualists without a heart',[38] without the power to resist and literally without a core, are now, in a literal and metaphorical sense, 'put into motion' and dependence by a bureaucratic structure of domination. Taken together, these two trends result in the null hypothesis for which Weber, in his scholarly work as well as his personal life,[39] was seeking a possible *non*-confirmation (in aesthetic, erotic, religious but above all in political spheres of life), with passionate and at the same time tragic interest.

Anyone who has ever opened *Economy and Society*, a work weighing more than a kilo, yet in many places sketchy and incomplete and never prepared for publication by its author, will remember that it is certainly not light reading. Any narrative or anecdotal element is foreign to the text, as the author seeks with the utmost effort and concentration to impose a typological order on the innumerable forms and phenomena of economic, legal, political and religious life. All the more striking is the (I believe) only anecdote with which Weber entertains us twice[40] and then once again

---

[36] 'This all-important economic fact: the "separation" of the worker from the material means of production, administration, academic research, and finance in general is the common basis of the modern state, in its political, cultural and military sphere, and of the private capitalist economy' (ES, Appendix II, 1394).

[37] 'Politics as a Vocation', in Weber 1958d, 113.

[38] PE, 182.

[39] See Mitzman 1971 and Krüger 2001.

[40] ES, 271; 'Politics as a Vocation', 110.

in the lecture on socialism.[41] The event on which it is based stayed in his memory for over sixteen years. Looking back in 1920, he reports an encounter he had on his American journey in 1904:

> As late as the early 1900s the author inquired of American workers of English origin why they allowed themselves to be governed by party henchmen who were so often open to corruption. The answer was, in the first place, that in such a big country even though millions of dollars were stolen or embezzled there was still plenty left for everybody, and secondly that these professional politicians were a group which even workers could treat with contempt whereas technical officials of the German type would as a group 'lord it over' the workers.[42]

This is explained by the defiant desire not to be dictated to, that 'magic of freedom' which, since the Freiburg inaugural lecture, he regarded as a 'primitive idealism', 'one of the most elemental drives in the human breast'.[43] The freedom theme constitutes *the* central problem of his whole work. In the constitutional political writings of 1918 the principal question is still formulated like this: 'Given the basic fact of the irresistible advance of bureaucratization . . . how can one possibly save *any remnants* of "individualist" freedom?'[44]

I can make only a few remarks here about Weber's concept of freedom, *the* central concept counterposed to soullessness, expropriation, proletarianization, dependence, professional specialization, and so on.[45] In comparison with Tocqueville's concept, Weber's is strictly individualistic ('individual freedom of movement'), and any sign of the republican ideal of moral and cognitive self-determination by a political community has been erased. Accordingly, it remains opaque which norms or principles are followed by those enjoying

---

[41] 'Socialism', in Weber 1994, 277.
[42] ES, 271.
[43] 'Nation State', in Weber 1994, 8.
[44] ES, 1403.
[45] On this subject, see Gneuss and Kocka 1988, 155–83.

their freedom. Wolfgang Mommsen has spoken of Weber as a 'liberal in despair'.[46] Since the application of human reason, on the one hand, and the utility of increasing prosperity, on the other, have been discarded as lodestars of bourgeois freedom,[47] the exercise of freedom has been transformed into an expression of the individual person that is authentic but can be neither imposed on others nor verified and comprehended by them – a dedicated commitment (to whatever)[48] that becomes a defining value of the individual. Weber adopts an activist perspective and conceptualizes freedom as an enhanced intensity of life activity, as heroic resistance, rebellion, dedication. The praxis of freedom, especially in political life, is, according to Weber, reserved for the few, because 'anyway, in a tense situation only a small committee can advise on and prepare truly *political* decisions.'[49] The suggestive formulations Weber uses to define the personal ethos of freedom are well known: 'responsibility', 'passion', 'objectivity', 'dedication', 'judgement', 'maturity', 'power', 'decency', 'cultivation', 'vocation', 'personal gift', 'nobility', 'greatness', 'the quality of humanity', 'manliness', 'character', 'clarity' and of course 'charisma' – all qualities of 'personality',[50] which works on its 'conduct of life' from 'inside out' and 'with the entire soul', is strong enough to withstand 'the ethical irrationality of the world',[51] and resists the 'parcellization of the soul'. For all that, it remains obscure who is being freed 'from' what or indeed 'for' what.[52]

---

[46] Mommsen 1974a, 95ff.

[47] In relation to the 'common good' and the utilitarian construction of social order, this dismissal already appears in the inaugural lecture of 1895. See GPS, 1–25.

[48] On the following, see also Hecht 1998, 212–15.

[49] Weber, *Gesamtausgabe*,15, 492.

[50] In Kamphausen's apt interpretation: 'The individual protest against the troublesome fact of having to conform to the rules of social order' (Kamphausen 2002, 212).

[51] 'Politics as a Vocation', 122.

[52] Cf. Lassman's apt critique of this rather Nietzschean version of Machiavelli's *virtù*: 'Ethical judgement enters into the political world by

The less clear the inner *content* of the '*daemon*' that structures and directs the 'free' person's way of life, the more it becomes a matter of the social *procedures* by which persons achieve not only formal authority but also the qualifications for (leading) positions and access to power and life chances. These social procedures are for Weber those of 'selection' or 'breeding'. 'The proper selection of political leadership',[53] Marianne Weber correctly sums up, 'was to Weber the most important problem of parliamentarianism and democratization.'[54] In general, the concept of selection used in this sense, of which there are dozens of examples in *Economy and Society*, has to do with the 'latent'[55] selection mechanisms in society (such as oracles, drawing lots, monopolistic restrictions, election, appointment, combat, competition centred on the market or personal achievement, qualification certificates, and so on). These rules of selection for life chances and access to power lead to 'adaptation', that is, to formative effects which result from the efforts of actors to conform to the dominant rules of selection and to achieve or maintain their life chances. At the same time, these rules themselves – as Weber demonstrates with the example of 'closure' – can be changed or preserved in pursuit of material or non-material interests. Weber (for the most part carefully avoiding any biologistic associations)[56] describes the interaction between

    means of [Weber's] idea of the genuine political leader. . . . To what is the
    political leader responsible? . . . [I]t might be said that there is a respon-
    sibility to history and fate. . . . but such talk is inherently vague and . . .
    contradicts his own methodological prescriptions' (Lassman 1993, 112).

[53] Weber's criterion for the 'right' manner of selection cannot be examined
    further here. A closer examination would probably reveal that Weber
    has in mind *two* criteria: on the one hand, fairness and impartiality and,
    on the other, the kind of selection process that consists of a rigorous,
    intensive, challenging and prolonged test of the candidate's personal
    character. See Mommsen 1984, 396ff.

[54] Marianne Weber 1975, 586.

[55] ES, 38f.

[56] The centrality of both these concepts in Weber's thought is also
    reflected in the title of the study undertaken by the Verein für
    Socialpolitik (Association for Social Policy) in industrial sociology,

selection and adaptation[57] as 'breeding', as in the formulation 'the breeding of professionalism'.[58]

In the example of the American sects (and their secular derivatives, such as clubs and other voluntary associations), Weber discovered a unique mechanism for which he introduced the concept of selection by ballot (*Ballotage*). This concept, used by him only in connection with American conditions,[59] represents for Weber quite simply *the* central reproduction mechanism of the 'Yankee' social character that he clearly admires. The principle of voluntary[60] membership within self-governing associations, religious sects as well as secular clubs, means that admission has the effect of 'legitimating [a member's] personal qualifications'[61] to the world, because he has obviously 'measured up to the congregation's religious and moral standards'.[62]

There are striking similarities in this respect between Tocqueville's explanation of American 'habits of the heart' or ways of thinking and Weber's explanation of the American social character. This has led a number of authors to suspect that Weber owed a greater debt to Tocqueville than one might suppose from his consistent failure to mention the young French aristocrat who had travelled to the United States seventy-three years before him. Marianne Weber in 1939 went so far as to write to J. P. Mayer, the editor of Tocqueville's work: 'La parenté spirituelle entre les vues historiques et sociologiques des deux penseurs me semble

---

which he initiated: 'Auslese und Anpassung . . . der Arbeiterschaft' ('Selection and Adaptation . . . of Workers'). SSP, 1–60.

[57] 'Nation State', 10.

[58] ES, 1200.

[59] See ES, 1206; SSP, 491; 'Sects', 307.

[60] 'Voluntary' means that the members *decide* on admission, that membership is granted by *decision* after an examination of the candidate's qualities, and members can also *decide* to exclude a member in response to some kind of transgression. '[A] fairly reputable sect would only accept for membership one whose "conduct" made him appear to be morally *qualified* beyond doubt' ('Sects', 305).

[61] ES, 1205.

[62] Ibid.

une chose très plausible.'[63] Nevertheless, in the absence of any evidence in Weber's writings (or even in his letters), it must remain an object of speculation whether Tocqueville's admiration for the social and moral resources that enable Americans to resist the freedom-destroying effects of modernization and mass society are directly echoed in Weber's portrait of America. The same is certainly true of the thesis of Loader and Alexander, at any rate its conclusion: 'What did Weber see in America that stimulated him so? We believe that it was a glimmer of a way out of the "iron cage" of reified modern society.'[64] Weber's admiration for the mode of selection and adaptation arising out of sectarian life in America becomes strikingly clear when, immediately after the end of the First World War, he reflects on possible ways to achieve the 'moral regeneration of the nation' and the 'restoration of respectability . . . as the basis of bourgeois economic life'[65] and, in a still unpublished letter, recommends:

> The means: the American 'club' and associations of every kind based on *selective* choice of members, starting with childhood and youth, no matter what the [association's] goals.[66]

Weber's ambivalence and uncertainty about the role the American social model might play in Europe becomes evident, however, if we contrast this forceful advice with a point he made twelve years earlier under the relatively fresh impressions of his American journey. This also appears in a letter (with which he curtly and certainly not unintentionally provoked the recipient, the Lutheran theologian Adolf Harnack, who had also attended the congress in St Louis):

[63] 'The spiritual kinship between the historical and sociological views of the two thinkers seems to me very plausible' (quoted in French from Freund 1974, 457). For more evidence and reflections on Tocqueville's influence on Weber, see Hennis 1995; Hecht 1998; Lassman 1993, 99ff.; Portinaro 2001, 292.

[64] Loader and Alexander 1985.

[65] Mommsen 1984, 323.

[66] Letter to Crusius, 24 November 1918, quoted from Mommsen 1984, 323; emphasis in the original.

The time for 'sects' or anything essentially like them is . . . historically past. But the fact that our nation has never gone through the
school of hard asceticism in *any* form is . . . the source of everything I find odious in it (and in myself), and, particularly judged in
religious terms . . . the average member of an American sect simply
. . . stands far above the 'Christians' of our national church.[67]

Weber regarded with admiration the puritanical asceticism
of American sects and thought of it as a revolutionary force,
as the energy source of the American dynamic, which, to be
sure, had by this time run out. In another letter to the same
recipient he writes:

> we owe to the sects things that none of us today can do without,
> the freedom of conscience and elementary human rights which
> today we take for granted.[68]

Puritan sectarianism created in those imbued with its spirit
a self-conscious, individualistic and sober attitude to life that
confronted state power with an anti-authoritarian scepti-
cism.[69] Weber was convinced that this moral syndrome of
freedom flourished only as long it could be exercised in the
independent and creative crossing of a *frontier* and the constant encounter with a new challenge. For Weber, the end of
that challenge was looming and with it the fall of the Puritan
ethic. 'Considered in human terms . . . this is the last time
in human history that such conditions for a free and great
development exist; free territories are now disappearing
throughout the world.'[70]

In what follows I shall look more closely at four spheres
of life in the United States that Weber regards with
deep ambivalence, with 'remarkable ambiguity'.[71] On the one
hand, he is impressed because they seem to him reserves for

---

[67] Letter to Adolf Harnack, 5 February 1906, Weber, *Gesamtausgabe*, II/5,
33; emphasis in original.
[68] Letter to Harnack, 12 January 1905, quoted from Mommsen 1974b, 76.
[69] Mommsen 1974b, 82.
[70] Weber 1952, 452.
[71] Kamphausen 2002, 182, 265ff.

that 'magic of freedom', while at the same time – in keeping with his own views about the threats to freedom from the destructive and secularizing tendencies of 'occidental rationalism' – he wants to show that, sooner or later, they will most likely fall victim to an overpowering 'Europeanization' and take the familiar main path of rationalization. These spheres of life are public administration, political parties, associations in civil society, and the university.

(1) *Public administration and the court system*   In his historical comparative sociology of state administration, Weber explains that the achievement of administration through a full-time bureaucratic staff is unavoidable (hence 'bureaucracy is our destiny'), because a traditional, politicized or amateur (self-) administration is simply inadequate to the functional demands of the modern state.[72] This also applies to the court system, which must be run by elected professionally trained and certified jurists appointed to their positions, not by lay judges.[73] 'It is in general not possible to attain a high level of technical

---

[72] According to the argument of the 'convergence theory' about the Europeanization of America, there is a 'development of modern officialdom into a highly qualified, professional labour force, specialized in expertness through long years of preparatory training . . . [which] in the interest of integrity has developed a high sense of status honour; without this sense the danger of an awful corruption and vulgar Philistinism threatens fatally. And without such integrity, even the purely technical functions of the state apparatus would be endangered . . . .. In the United States, amateur administration through booty politicians in accordance with the outcome of presidential elections resulted in the exchange of hundreds of thousands of officials, even down to the mail carrier. The administration knew nothing of the professional civil-servant-for-life, but this amateur administration has long since been punctured by the Civil Service Reform. Purely technical, irrefragable needs of the administration have determined this development' ('Politics as a Vocation', 87–8). In his reflections on the United States, Weber is always on the lookout for signs or premonitions of secularization, bureaucratization and a neo-feudal aristocratization of American society.

[73] 'Whatever form law and legal practice may come to assume under the impact of various influences, it will be inevitable that, as a result of technical and economic developments, the legal ignorance of the layman will

administrative efficiency with an elected staff of officials.'[74]
But Weber suddenly concedes, in light of his American impressions, that there does exist a type of 'leaderless democracy',
which 'is characterized by the attempt to minimize the domination of man over man.'[75] He thus sees here a weakening of
the bureaucratizing impulse, even if at the price of a more
limited decisiveness and efficiency in public administration.
That kind of administration 'is greatly inferior as a precision
instrument compared to the bureaucratic type with its
appointed officials'[76] – though this can and must be accepted
in America, he seems to be saying. In the end he leaves it open
what price should be paid in administrative dilettantism and
inconsistency in return for 'direct' or 'immediate' democracy.[77]
Weber, to be sure, holds the view that the European-style 'official' (*Beamter*), in comparison with elected office-holders,
'normally functions, from a technical point of view, more
accurately';[78] but that in the United States – voice-over
Tocqueville: 'Americans commit faults which they may afterwards repair' – this advantage can also be achieved by elected
officials, at least where people who acquire office by means of
party patronage 'have to take into account an intellectually
developed, educated, and free "public opinion".'[79]

In the end, Weber clearly decides in favour of the convergence and 'Europeanization' thesis in relation to public
administration. (In the process, he uncharacteristically makes

increase. The use of jurors and similar lay judges will not suffice to stop
the continuous growth of the technical elements in the law and hence
its character as a specialist's domain. Inevitably the notion must expand
that the law is a rational technical apparatus' (ES, 895).

[74] ES, 269.
[75] Ibid. He holds out the prospect of discussing this type in greater detail,
but this is not done in *Economy and Society* with any further reference
to the American case. But cf. ES, 290f., where Weber, referring to
'American townships', discusses the type of 'direct democracy' reminiscent of certain ideas of council socialism.
[76] ES, 267.
[77] ES, 289.
[78] ES, 960.
[79] ES, 961.

use of a word or phrase that evokes the notion of some trend, which I shall highlight in the following by inserting [*].)

> The United States still [*] bears the character of a polity which, at least in the technical sense, is not fully bureaucratized. But the greater the zones of friction with the outside and the more urgent the needs for administrative unity at home become, the more this character is inevitably [*] and gradually [*] giving way formally to the bureaucratic structure.[80] . . . The American Civil Service Reform movement gradually [*] imports expert training and specialized examinations into the United States, . . . from its [the examination system's] main breeding ground, Germany.[81]

The alternative to this is adherence to the 'elective principle' – and with it the power of 'municipal "dictators"'[82] and 'invisible cliques which . . . are highly irresponsible toward the public. The candidates are presented to voters who themselves have no capacity for technical judgment.'[83]

As to the court system, 'One can also still [*] observe the charismatic character of lawfinding', which manifests itself in 'the very personal authority of an individual judge . . . .. [I]n the American view, the judgment is the very personal creation of the concrete individual judge.'[84] 'In the popular American view, a judge's job is a business just as a banker's.'[85] He notes with some irritation that 'American adjudication by the highest courts is still [*] to a great extent empirical, and specifically: adjudication by precedents.'[86]

(2) *Political parties* Weber equates the organization and operation of political parties in America with those of European social democratic parties. They are turning into strictly bureaucratic organizations, if necessary with a

[80] ES, 971.
[81] ES, 999.
[82] ES, 268.
[83] ES, 1455.
[84] ES, 890.
[85] ES, 947.
[86] ES, 976.

charismatic 'hero' or otherwise with a political manager or 'boss' at the top.[87] At the centre of this, for Weber unusually sarcastic, portrayal of the American party system is the 'job patronage party' and the figure of the corrupt, unprincipled and despicable 'boss', who plans and conducts elections as major investments, so that, if successful, he can recover the costs from those he puts into office or those he helps by means of his own position in office.[88] This pure concentration on gaining power in the political 'market' and in electoral contests nevertheless has the advantage, Weber observes, of an unrestricted capacity for innovation.

> [T]he reception of new ideas proceeds relatively fast only there, where parties completely devoid of principles and devoted only to office patronage, as in the United States, add to their 'platforms' whichever 'planks' they think will gain them the most votes.[89]

In his portrayal of the American party system he leaves little doubt that this 'business' method of leadership selection runs counter to his own ethical principles – but without making any predictions about its further development or elimination. Since he has categorically rejected (though with a conciliatory glance at Swiss cantons) all but the elite-minoritarian forms of domination 'in mass states', such as politics conducted by honoraries and notables, collegial leadership, forms of 'direct' democracy, and so on, the only remaining way out is the parliamentarization of government, which he does then recommend for Germany. With respect to parties and party politics, at any rate, he finds nothing that could make the idea of an 'Americanization' of European conditions either attractive or likely.

(3) *Sects and associations*   Weber's judgement on the life of religious communities and corresponding secular associations

---

[87] ES, 1131–2f.
[88] Cf. ES, 1429–30, 1447, 1458; SSP, 405.
[89] ES, 1458.

in the United States is significantly more sober than
Tocqueville's. He is concerned less with the disappearance of
these local forms of 'associative action' in civil society than
with their insidious changes of function.[90] Weber sees
more clearly than Tocqueville, with his admiration for the
American 'art of association', that these forms of association
do not (any longer) serve as schools for the common good or
as correctives to competitive individualism but are themselves already implicated in the system of competing economic interests. At the same time, he sees within the sects
'the principle of the solidarity of brothers in the faith, which
under certain circumstances might bring the brotherliness
close to a communism of love. . . . Many of the secularized
organizations which have replaced the sects in the United
States still [*] make such claims upon their members.'[91] Yet
this ethos is disappearing, according to Weber, as a consequence of 'modern disintegration' [*].[92] He comes closest to
Tocqueville when he detects in American clubs a culture of
egalitarian respect among fellow citizens, which is granted
irrespective of status differences.[93]

He regards with coolness, however, the use of American
sects for economic ends: 'A person who wants to open a bank
joins the Baptists or Methodists, for everybody knows that
baptism, respectively admission, is preceded by an *examen rig-
orosum* which inquires about the blemishes in his past
conduct: frequenting an inn, sexual life, card playing, making

---

[90] 'American sects, for instance, arrange artistic, athletic and other entertainment . . . .. [R]eligious and political parties establish youth groups
and women's chapters and participate eagerly in purely municipal or
other basically non-political activities, which enable them to grant
economic favour to local private interests' (ES, 347).

[91] ES, 581–2.

[92] 'Sects', 308.

[93] '[I]t would be considered strictly repugnant . . . if even the richest boss,
while playing billiards or cards in his club, would not treat his clerk as
in every sense fully his equal in birthright, but would bestow upon him
the condescending status-conscious "benevolence" which the German
boss can never dissever from his attitude' (ES, 932).

debts, other levities, insincerity, etc.; if the result of the inquiry is positive, creditworthiness is guaranteed.'[94] As we have seen, membership in sects, as distinct from churches, functions through the mechanisms of selection and adaptation as an 'absolute guarantee of the moral qualities of a gentleman, especially of those qualities required in business matters',[95] because of the voluntary nature of both joining and acceptance. In his sociology of religion, Weber cites at several points the principle 'honesty is the best policy',[96] adding that this is a principle of 'early capitalism'. In these early capitalist conditions, where honesty in business is, to be sure, rewarded by wealth yet is not practised for the sake of wealth but purely to meet the requirements of the religious life, citizens discover, as it were to their own pleasant surprise, the utility of virtue:

> [T]he Christian sects of the seventeenth and eighteenth centuries (particularly the Baptists and Quakers) pointed with pride to the fact that precisely in economic intercourse with the godless they had substituted legality, honesty, and fairness for falseness, overreaching, and unreliability; . . . in short, that their superior, religiously determined economic ethics gave them superiority over the competition of the godless according to the principle 'honesty is the best policy'. This is in complete agreement with what could still [*] be concretely discerned in the United States during recent decades as characteristic of the middle class way of life.[97]

Since those heroic days of early capitalism, there has been, according to Weber, a gradual reversal[98] of motives: it is no longer the intrinsic value of the religious life itself that motivates the membership of Protestant sects and the

---

[94] ES, 1206.
[95] 'Sects', 305.
[96] PE, 282 n. 12; 'Sects', 13; Weber 1962, 344.
[97] Weber 1962, 344.
[98] A reversal which, as he says, is 'irrational from the normal point of view' (GARS 1, 35; cf. PE, 53); see Weber's repeated discussion of this central problem with reference to the autobiography of Benjamin Franklin in PE, 48–56.

content of their precepts but rather the pursuit of an external reputation which membership confers on members as a 'qualification certificate' in business matters. Despite this function on behalf of business interests and the disillusioning admixture of plutocratic and neo-aristocratic mechanisms of selection in American associations and clubs, Weber sees in the 'sects and their derivatives' a strong element of free individualism,[99] even if this phenomenon 'is often in the process of rotting away [*]', in addition to social integration into 'communities' and also quasi-status stratification: 'American democracy is not a sand-pile of unrelated individuals but a maze of highly exclusive, yet absolutely voluntary sects, associations and clubs, which provide the centre of the individual's social life.'[100] Weber sees here a 'very intense church-mindedness', which nonetheless used to be [*] 'even far stronger' and 'unquestioned'.[101] Although 'today they are decaying' [*], he regards their 'derivatives, rudiments and survivals'[102] as bearers of that moral energy which has led to the 'breeding' of the 'ascetist professional ethic' and the ethos of the 'methodical, rational way of life' of the 'modern bourgeois middle class' – and which is lacking in 'churches' of the European type (especially the Lutheran).[103]

(4) *University life*—Weber's visits to Northwestern University (Evanston, Illinois) and Harvard, as well as Bryn Mawr and Haverford colleges in Pennsylvania, fascinated him because of the 'scholarly education' and personality formation practised there.[104] Study there had its own intrinsic scholarly value and was not preparation for a career.[105] He clearly regards the

---

[99] Kamphausen 2002, 205.
[100] ES, 1207f.; similarly, 'Sects', 309, and SSP, 443.
[101] 'Sects', 302–3; again the suggestion of a trend towards secularization (cf. ibid., 307) and Europeanization, which Weber attributes to the flood of European immigrants.
[102] Ibid., 319f.
[103] Ibid., 312, 321.
[104] Letter, 27 October 1904, quoted from Scaff 1998, 75.
[105] Cf. Busch 1959.

universities as scholarly derivatives of sectarian socialization. In the academic institutions too, as in the American example generally, he sees the development of big business forms and bureaucratic structures. Whereas in Germany there was the '*Privatdozent*', who (at that time still) had a private income and his own research library – i.e. he had to be 'plutocratically' 'selected' and, moreover, depended on the personal protection of the professoriate for promotion to their ranks – in the United States a comparable position was filled by a professionally examined assistant, who was appointed to his position and paid for his work, could be dismissed, and depended on his employer for the material means of his occupation (laboratory, library, etc.). Weber wants to say: plutocracy or bureaucracy – *tertium non datur* (least of all the alternative of a dilettantish self-administration by notables, with their 'vanities', which Weber sharply condemned). 'Democracy offers only one choice: it can be run either cheaply by rich people in honorary positions or expensively by paid officials.'[106] Bureaucratization in the state and in scholarship are necessary to the extent that the universities are increasingly becoming big business enterprises, largely because of the demand of the state for professionally trained officials and functionaries. Weber also wants to say: better the latter, bureaucracy – in particular, in his lecture 'Science as a Vocation', his account of American university life is remarkably positive.

'German university life is being Americanized'[107] – and this to its benefit! Weber is here elaborating the egalitarian aspect of bureaucratic forms. 'The young American has no respect for anything or anybody, for tradition or for public office – unless it is for the personal achievement of individual men. This is what the American calls "democracy." . . . The American's conception of the teacher who faces him is: he

---

[106] SSP, 495.
[107] 'Science as a Vocation', in Weber 1958d, 131; this thought – repeated in the 'Socialism' lecture – is the only one in Weber's work in which the 'Americanization' of European conditions is not only asserted but also unmistakably welcomed.

sells me his knowledge and his methods'.[108] German students, by contrast, 'come to our lectures and demand from us the qualities of leadership'[109] and readily confuse the professor with a 'leader to give directions in practical life'. It is well known that Weber had an intense distaste for the expectation in Germany that professors should impart to students inspirational guidance on the conduct of life. This also explains the profound if paradoxical value that he attaches to value-free scholarship. '[D]ilettantism as a leading principle would be the end of science. He who yearns for "show" should go to the cinema'.[110] He insists that 'the academic lecture-hall achieves a really valuable influence only through specialized training by specially qualified persons. For the latter, therefore, "intellectual integrity" is the only specific virtue which it should seek to inculcate.'[111]

As concerns these reflections on his own sphere of activity, that of organized scholarship, three mirror images immediately stand out. First, the American bureaucratization of higher education (although 'only in its beginnings'[112] [*]) is opposed to the German system, which is pre-bureaucratic, based on corporative and dilettantish self-government and a more or less plutocratic system. Second, Weber makes it unmistakably clear that the American system and the 'spirit' it produces in young people are to be preferred. And third, if I am not mistaken, this is the only place in the whole of his work where Weber identifies a tendency not to the Europeanization of America but to the Americanization of Europe.

In Tocqueville, we saw an argument that Europe is a long way from Americanization, i.e. a breakthrough to 'democracy' and a progressive reconciliation of equality and freedom. In favourable circumstances America has overtaken

[108] Ibid., 149.
[109] Ibid., 150.
[110] PE, 29; translation modified.
[111] 'The Meaning of Ethical Neutrality in Sociology and Economics', in Weber 1949, 3.
[112] 'Science as a Vocation', 149.

Europe, which is hopelessly impeded by its historical legacies. In Weber, for all his particular ambiguities, the dominant argument is: America is for the moment 'still' backward in a favourable sense, because, and as long as, it has 'free territories'[113] at its disposal; but, in the absence of any respectable and practicable alternative in modern mass society, it is in the process of 'Europeanizing' its now plutocratically deformed traditions of civil society and self-government.[114]

Today, after the end of a threat to the 'West' as perceived on both sides of the Atlantic, the convergence hypothesis implicit in Weber's question – whether we are dealing with an Americanization of Europe or a Europeanization of America – hardly seems relevant any more. On the one hand, after two world wars as well as the Cold War, there are scarcely any persuasive grounds for the 'Europeanization of America' thesis. Even at the time of the Kosovo intervention in 1999, Europe depended on the United States above all for military force, which European nation-states, both individually and collectively, have been unable to generate. Europe's history of dependence upon American help has obviously reduced the chances that the European model will serve in the USA itself as a standard for American development. But, even apart from that, in the twentieth century social, political and cultural structures developed in the United States which distanced it ever further from Europe (and even from its Canadian neighbours, who are much more shaped by Europe). The ethnic composition of the American people and the languages and traditions non-European immigrants have brought with them, as well as specific US-American political, economic and social structures, states and regions, military and foreign policy, media, scientific and religious life, have produced an ever greater independence and divergence from corresponding European institutions, which

---

[113] Weber 1952, 452.
[114] The comparative literature on the two American journeys is neither extensive nor particularly rich. See above all Diggins 1996a, Lassman 1993, Freund 1974, Kalberg 2000.

is increasingly removing any empirical grounds for the notion of an analogous modernization process on both sides of the Atlantic. Conversely, we can speak of an 'Americanization' of Europe only in the most limited sense, as a history of military dependence, economic interdependence and American cultural influences has given Europe a significant motive for creating a supranational European independence and identity. The link of the 'Occident' (as we have seen, a geographically somewhat imprecise notion in Weber's work), the essential similarity of American and European societies identified by Weber, has been significantly weakened from both sides. This is demonstrated not only by the current American situation but also – despite the continued existence of NATO – by the substantially expanded ambitions on our side of the Atlantic, brought about by European integration, to establish a kind of international regime that is fundamentally different from the American one.

4
Theodor W. Adorno: 'Culture Industry' and Other Views of the 'American Century'

The question of which interpretations of European trends emerged from Adorno's American experience can be meaningfully answered only if we take into account the fundamental differences between his stay in the United States and the trips of Tocqueville and Weber. These differences are obvious enough. Adorno did not go 'of his own free will', to study the country and to gather information; he was forced to emigrate from Nazi Germany and, after a first stop in Oxford, ended up in America in precarious material circumstances, through the good offices of Max Horkheimer. Adorno saw the United States not with the eyes of a field researcher or travelling academic, but with those of a refugee. This is connected with a second difference: if we leave aside his only 'voluntary' crossing of the Atlantic, a one-year trip in 1952–3 that would be his last, the period of his major stay (February 1938 to November 1949) came to a full eleven years. This contrasts with the third difference: despite the long time he spent in America, and despite the fact that he had incomparably better travel conditions, Adorno made only one brief stop in Chicago en route to Los Angeles[1] and visited

[1] Müller-Doohm 2005, 417ff.

few other cities;[2] otherwise, he travelled only on holidays to relax amid attractive scenery. His two longer stays were in the two coastal metropolises: New York (1938–41) and Los Angeles (1942–49).

All three of these differences considerably affected Adorno's image of America and its applications to the study of contemporary European society. In comparison with Alexis de Tocqueville and Max Weber, Adorno's intellectual interest in cultural and social conditions in the United States was narrow and selective.[3] He occupied himself with research projects *in* the United States and individual aspects of American culture and society, not with research or investigations *about* the United States. Of course, he did become thoroughly familiar with living conditions there, and his work after the 1940s is filled with expressions drawn from the language of everyday American life. But one has to go to a country of one's own free will, not as a refugee, in order to develop the kind of panoramic vision that we have encountered in our other two travellers. In any event, during his eleven years in the United States, Adorno saw far fewer places, and surveyed or commented on far fewer aspects of the American political system in particular, than Tocqueville in nine months or Weber in just thirteen weeks.

Above all else, the United States was for Adorno 'the country where I was saved';[4] he owed to it 'his salvation from Nazi persecution' and 'always kept in mind this existential debt of gratitude'.[5] Despite this feeling, however, the depression associated with the fate of an émigré did not leave him: he complains of it in many reports about himself, and it forms

---

[2] In his *Briefe an die Eltern*, Adorno describes Miami as 'terrible' (2003, 59) and 'one of the ghastliest places I've ever seen' (46), and St Louis as a 'dreadful big city' (53); and he speaks generally of the 'horror' of American cities (80), 'populated by drugstores, hot dogs and automobiles' (55). Chicago too left a 'quite dreadful impression' on him (107).

[3] Thus, he referred only rarely to Tocqueville's writings and conclusions about the United States, and not at all to those of Max Weber.

[4] Claussen 2003, 245, 256.

[5] Söllner 2003.

the experiential backdrop[6] to his 'Reflections from Damaged Life'.[7] Although he was naturalized an American citizen in 1943, he never assumed an American 'identity'.

These biographical conditions and orientations of the émigré period have their origin in the restrictions which – we should suspect – tormented Adorno more than others among the (mostly transitory but in some cases permanent) settlers of 'German California'. Being less well established than they, and less recognized, he suffered more as a result of his precarious work and income situation defined by temporary and (at least in the New York years) not freely chosen occupational activity. Already in Oxford, his first stop on the road of exile, he experienced major problems of adjustment and acutely felt his position as an outsider;[8] he wrote to Horkheimer that he had made 'profound loneliness . . . an a priori' of his life.[9] He was also tortured by his linguistic handicap, which meant that in an English-speaking environment he did not have such a sensitive and skilful command of words as in his mother tongue. 'Terrible sadness', 'melancholy' and 'homesickness' are the terms that Lorenz Jäger uses in his political biography to describe this period.[10] Often noted too is the ten-year-long 'cultural shock' with which the European middle-class intellectual reacted to the impositions of everyday life in America. 'Every visit to the cinema leaves me, against all my vigilance, stupider and worse', is how he recorded one affecting experience.[11] There was also the philosophical despair,[12] so to speak, that it would never be

---

6 Already in 1939, in a letter to his parents, Adorno described himself (referring to Kürnberger) as 'weary of America' (2003, 18), and later he spoke of his 'general state of depression' due to 'the complete insecurity of conditions here' (131). 'I remain highly unsuited to the life of an émigré' (143).

7 The subtitle of Adorno's *Minima Moralia*.

8 Jäger 2004, 88.

9 Adorno and Horkheimer, 2003, 374.

10 Jäger 2004, chap. 9.

11 Adorno, 1978, 25.

12 Ibid., 247.

possible to define a practical or even theoretical basis for
redemption and reconciliation in the face of the entrenched
conditions of American society, with its totalitarian tendencies and its social character shaped by the culture industry,
and that he found himself forced to learn to live with the
'superior might of the existent'[13] without falsely consenting
to it. And there was also the terror about the 'unspeakable
collective events',[14] the Nazi annihilation of the Jews, and,
given the perceived virulence of anti-Semitism in the USA,
the fear that it might continue there. 'Life does not live' was
the motto he placed at the beginning of *Minima Moralia*.[15]
He also used his own experience of loneliness and homesickness for his diagnosis of the age, as in his interpretation of a
poem by Heine: 'Today, however, after the destiny that Heine
felt has literally become reality, homesickness has become the
homesickness of all; everyone is as damaged in their being and
language as outcasts used to be.'[16]

Throughout his period in America, Adorno operated
mainly within the network of European émigrés. Apart
from his uncommonly close collaboration with Horkheimer
and Leo Löwenthal, it was the community of 'German
California',[17] in many ways divided but also held together by
the issues, criteria and political-theoretical disputes it had
brought with it from Europe, which constituted the core of
Adorno's communicative existence. Nor is this surprising,
especially as that community consisted of figures who were

---

[13] Ibid., 25.
[14] Ibid., 18.
[15] This was a quotation made in all innocence from *Der Amerika-Müde*, a
novel by Ferdinand Kürnberger published in 1855, which Dan Diner
(2002, 35) quite accurately describes as an 'America-phobic diatribe
intensified by German jingoism and racist views'. In a late essay he wrote
in 1968, 'Scientific Experiences of a Scholar in America' (which, on the
whole, indicates a much milder judgement on American cultural and
academic conditions than the one contained in *Minima Moralia* – see
below), Adorno refers to Tocqueville and Kürnberger in the same breath
(1969, 369).
[16] Adorno, *Noten zur Literatur*, GS 11, 101.
[17] Claussen 2003, 152.

quite able to capture his attention and to focus his efforts to gain recognition for his theoretical and aesthetic achievements from people who were mostly his elders: people such as Thomas and Heinrich Mann, Fritz Lang, Ludwig Marcuse, Hanns Eisler, Bertolt Brecht, Arnold Schönberg, Igor Stravinsky, Fred Pollock, Alfred Döblin and Felix Weil.

The other side of these relations of communication and cooperation (for example, with Thomas Mann in the work on *Doctor Faustus* or with Hanns Eisler on their joint *Komposition für den Film*) was the émigré's equally persistent lack of interest in the specific cultural and intellectual production or the social and political conditions of the United States. The situation of black Americans, the New Deal way of tackling the economic and social crisis, urban, industrial and demographic trends in 1940s America, the entry of the United States into the war, the court system, trade unions, religious life including the problem of secularization: all these might have been expected to attract the attention of a social theorist concerned with the diagnosis of his times. It might also have been possible to link up with the sometimes quite similar efforts and achievements in contemporary American philosophy and social science (Robert S. Lynd, the Chicago School, C. Wright Mills, Thorstein Veblen, Talcott Parsons, James Dewey and pragmatism, David Riesman), and with distinctively American aesthetic products in music (apart from jazz, which Adorno emphatically rejected as worthless), cinema and architecture. Yet, to the extent that he had any contact at all with contemporary (or indeed historical) intellectual and aesthetic phenomena in the United States, it was highly selectively geared to the collection of evidence for his emerging theory of the culture industry, while the image he formed of American philosophical pragmatism, for example, remained at best a caricature.[18]

The vehemence and sometimes extreme agitation with which Adorno spoke of his American experiences should be understood, however, not only as a reflex to a biographical

[18] Joas 1993.

situation of agonizing isolation and uncertainty, but also as a method resulting from his radically anti-positivist concept of experience. This concept, with which he marked the difference between 'the expert technicians and the European "intellectual" ',[19] led him to make judgements such as those concerning jazz,[20] which predate any experience of America and which, not only from today's vantage-point, should be considered 'manifestly absurd'.[21] As far as the concept of experience is concerned, he speaks in the previously mentioned place of 'a kind of vindication of experience against its translation into empirical terms'[22] and outlines the alternative approach he had already consistently applied in *Minima Moralia*.[23] Even the minutest particles of social life – for example, a second-long interaction in the subway[24] – counted for him as opportunities to establish 'closest contact' with the 'materials' of theory.[25] Since such particles may be taken as unmistakable evidence of the entire structure of exchange and delusion of the administered world, protest and outrage are directed not against those particles alone but – and this would explain the surplus of rhetoric – against that world in its totality. 'The melting-pot was introduced by unbridled

---

[19] Adorno 1969, 350.
[20] One example is the article 'Über Jazz', which he published in 1936 under the pen name Hektor Rottweiler.
[21] Jäger 2004, 95.
[22] Adorno 1969, 370.
[23] Although at least once in *Minima Moralia* (1978, 67) harsh self-criticism leaves this approach in a state of aporia.
[24] See Adorno, 'Kein Abenteuer', GS 20.2, 585f.
[25] Adorno, 1969, 370. Adorno explains in *Minima Moralia* (1978, 80) what he means by this 'intimate contact' and the cognitive gain from it: 'Knowledge comes to us through a network of prejudices, opinions, innervations, self-corrections, presuppositions and exaggerations, in short through the dense, firmly founded but by no means uniformly transparent medium of experience.' By contrast, experience is cut to size by empiricism, and actually rendered inaccessible, if it is methodically checked and quantified and thereby subsumed under what, for Adorno, is the logic of 'administrative' social research and therefore itself part of the praxis of the culture industry.

industrial capitalism. The thought of being cast into it con-
jures up martyrdom, not democracy.'[26] 'Every married couple
appearing together is comic.'[27] If such assertions have any
truth-value, it rests not on their propositional content but on
the dazzlingly expressive linguistic gestures with which an
experience assumes the right to make itself heard – 'in accordance with the maxim that nowadays only exaggeration is
ever the medium of truth.'[28]

By themselves, the precarious and oppressive conditions of
émigré life can scarcely explain why Adorno's extremely harsh
criticism of cultural conditions and trends in his host country
had almost no equivalent in a critique of economics, distribu-
tive relations, military strategies and events (Hiroshima
and Nagasaki make only a very marginal appearance)[29] or
government policy (e.g. McCarthyism) in the United States.[30]

---

[26] Adorno, 1978, 103.

[27] Ibid., 173.

[28] Adorno, 'Was bedeutet: Aufarbeitung der Vergangenheit', GS 10.2, 567.

[29] 'By the way', he wrote to his parents on 19 August 1945, 'what do you
say about the atom bomb?' But he did not express any view of his own,
except to remark furiously on a statement by one of the Nuremberg
defendants: 'When you hear that, you regret that the atom bomb was
not tried out on Germany' (Adorno 2003, 326, 339).

[30] As regards McCarthyism and the interrogation of European intellectuals by the House Un-American Activities Committee in connection
with 'Communist Infiltration of the Motion Picture Industry', Adorno
cautiously revoked his joint authorship of both the English (*Composing
for the Films*, 1947) and the German (*Komposition für den Film*, 1949 –
now in GS 15) editions of the book he wrote with (the communist)
Hanns Eisler and completed in 1944 – even though, as a naturalized US
citizen, he was by no means as subject to reprisals as Brecht or Eisler. 'I
had no reason to become a martyr for a cause that was not my own' (GS
15, 144; cf. Wiggershaus 1994, 390). In an 'editorial note', the editors of
the *Gesammelte Schriften* do not go into the details of this aspect of the
book's history, but they do mention that, in two letters from 1964 and
1965, Adorno recognized that he had himself written 95 or 90 per cent
of it. All the more excessive seems the fear that the author evidently felt
of 'guilt by association'; this induced him to cease claiming joint authorship of a work that was in its major part clearly his own. See also Adorno
2003, 407.

In contrast to the position taken by Herbert Marcuse, the critique of capitalism and imperialism became increasingly muted in the work of Adorno and Horkheimer:[31] on the one hand, they stuck to their radical formulation about the totalitarian tendencies in monopoly capitalism; on the other hand, apart from the complex case of *Dialectic of Enlightenment*, their use of such concepts was marked by a certain timidity. Adorno himself openly explained this reserve in terms of his plan at the time to return to the American-occupied zone of Germany: 'I feared anything that might stand in its way.'[32]

Which of the insights and convictions that Adorno took away from America might have served him as a key for the understanding of contemporary European reality? First of all, the European émigrés of the 1940s, unlike any previous generation, found themselves empty-handed in the face of the shocking reality of America: that is, without support in a positive European identity and its educated middle-class or cultural-aristocratic premises, for which 'the fundamental importance of the mind was . . . self-evident'.[33] Europe was now experiencing an acute form of barbarism, beside which – however great one's criticism of American capitalism and the culture industry – one could only give preference to the country where one was 'at a safe distance', and where Adorno had discovered 'a potential for real generosity that is seldom to be found in old Europe'.[34] In addition to the damage already done to European identity, there were the fateful tendencies visible in American reality and described in *Minima Moralia* and *Dialectic of Enlightenment* – tendencies that might spread to Europe from the more advanced American context, itself 'not immune from the danger of an upset in the

---

[31] See Rabinbach 1995, 115.

[32] Adorno, 'Zum Erstdruck der Originalfassung', GS 15, 144.

[33] Adorno 1969, 367.

[34] Ibid., 368. There is an abrupt and surprising change of tone in Adorno's remarks in the *Briefe an die Eltern* concerning the 'friendship and humanity' and the 'genuinely democratic spirit of helpfulness and cooperation' (2003, 132, 150) that he encountered among Americans donating blood and at the micro-level of social interactions.

direction of totalitarian forms of domination',[35] without the workers, or any other intellectual or political movement, being in a position to stop them.

A systematic account of how Adorno applied his experience of American social relations to the contemporary diagnosis of Europe has to deal with three issues. The first of these is the *truth content* of the generalizations that he and his fellow thinkers drew from the American experience.[36] The second is the question of whether they were themselves *consistent* and remained so in relation to Adorno's later work – or whether they held views (discernible at least as the implied premiss of their academic and non-academic work) which are simply incompatible with the two guiding ideas of Adorno's theory: social integration through the culture industry, and systemic integration resulting from pacification of the contradiction between productive forces and relations of production. In short, did the authors of critical theory act in the way that one would expect people to act who are convinced of the truth of that theory? Finally, the third question is whether for Adorno anything (and, if so, what) stood in the place that, for Tocqueville, and to some extent for Weber, was occupied by *internal contradictions*, ambivalences, salutary antidotes, countervailing tendencies, a set of self-correcting mechanisms offering the possibility of escape from the 'iron cage of dependence' and the 'administered world'. And, more particularly, was there anything in the realities of America that might serve as the basis for such mechanisms?

The suggestive power of closely observed American cultural practices (such as radio, jazz, film, horoscopes in the daily press, magazines and sport, but also positivistic social or 'administrative' research) led Adorno and Horkheimer to

[35] Adorno 1969, 367.

[36] To take just one example, the apodictic thesis concerning the culture industry must today face – and must have done so even then – serious counter-evidence, such as the films of Robert Altman (e.g. *Short Cuts*, in my view a grandiose film version of the very phenomena with which Adorno concerned himself in *Minima Moralia*) or the avant-garde jazz of Thelonious Monk and others.

develop a spectacularly influential and successful critical diagnosis of society. They took for granted the two trends of capitalist society rigidly fixed by Marxist orthodoxy – the development of competitive into monopoly capitalism, and the parallel development of liberal democracy into what Horkheimer called the 'authoritarian state' – and supplemented them with a third tendency: namely, the development of autonomous bourgeois culture into mass culture and the culture industry. This entailed a culturalist or social-psychological turn in social analysis, which meant that it was necessary to explain also at the level of cultural reproduction the seamless, and therefore 'totalitarian', integration of the members of Stalinist, fascist as well as nominally democratic societies. Central to this analysis was the idea that these societies grow stronger through propaganda for existing reality[37] and, for social-structural reasons (as shown in *Studien über Autorität und die Familie* and *The Authoritarian Personality*), bring to the fore ego-weak personality types without powers of cognitive or moral resistance, who are defenceless in the face of such propaganda.[38] 'What is being promulgated is general uncritical consensus.'[39] This also provides a key to the most urgent problem that left intellectuals had to face in the 1930s and 1940s: the failure of the workers' movement.[40] Here too Adorno considers American experiences to be of prognostic value: what is already evident in California is still to come in 'backward' Europe.[41] What for Tocqueville was still a means of defending autonomy – that is, the civil society of clubs, churches and associations – becomes for critical theory the agency of conformist *Gleichschaltung*. 'No one is officially responsible for what he thinks. Instead everyone is enclosed at an early age in a system of churches, clubs,

---

[37] Adorno, 'Résumé über Kulturindustrie', GS 10.1, 337–45.
[38] In *Briefe an die Eltern*, the talk is of 'psychologically crippled and white-collarized Americans' (2003, 78) and their 'barbaric half-civilization' (66).
[39] 'Résumé über Kulturindustrie', GS 10.1, 339.
[40] See Rabinbach 1995, 117.
[41] DoE, 132.

professional associations, and other such concerns, which constitute the most sensitive instrument of social control.'[42]

This is one thread of Adorno's diagnosis of advanced societies that he derived from his experiences in America. The other is a revision of the basic Marxist theorem concerning the contradiction between forces of production (hence gradual control over nature) and relations of production (hence social relations of power and inequality). According to that optimistic theorem of classical historical materialism, there is a whole series of paths along which advances in science and technology tend to reduce the degree of repression, making it gradually less 'necessary', and to promote human emancipation by overcoming not only material scarcity but also the lack of freedom bound up with the relations of production and political domination. These two sides of the Enlightenment are growing control over external nature and a critique of domination by the legitimatory yardstick of its declining necessity for the organization of economic life. The mutually reinforcing dynamic of these two potentials of human reason, which Marx saw as leading to a 'free association' of producers in place of the 'despotism of factory labour',[43] has in Adorno's view been brought to a standstill, so that greater freedom from natural constraints does not reduce but actually increases social power and control. 'On the one hand the growth of economic productivity furnishes the conditions for a world of greater justice; on the other hand it allows the technical apparatus and the social groups which administer it a disproportionate superiority to the rest of the population. The individual is wholly devalued in relation to the economic powers.'[44] The authors here speak of the 'absurdity of a state of affairs in which the power of the system over men grows with every step that takes them out of the power of nature.'[45]

[42] DoE, 149.
[43] Marx and Engels 1959–, 4.482; 16.11f.; 25.276, 456, 828.
[44] DoE, xiv.
[45] DoE, 38; translation modified.

What is transposed from America to an interpretation of the situation facing Europe is the terrifying vision of a possible convergence between 'European totalitarianism' and 'the American entertainments industry'.[46] Adorno is deeply convinced that fascism is 'a universal tendency', that 'America will inevitably take over crucial elements of fascism'; he considers the fascist 'threat here to be extremely serious' and, in a letter from July 1945, starts from the danger that the looming Cold War 'will push American capitalism in a fascist direction'.[47]

Adorno, then, is not so much interested in the United States as such, and certainly not in its genuine divergence from European patterns; rather, he uses it as the object of an *exemplary* critique, which refers to developed capitalist societies as a whole. His stay there is an opportunity to study, from 'the most advanced observation post',[48] the 'pure' and therefore clear case of developments that will just as thoroughly affect the rest of the world: the 'destruction of progress', the 'Janus face of reason', 'enlightenment as mass deception'. Looking back in 1968, he remains convinced that Europe is 'in harmony with the economic-technological trend' of a 'general tendency of society' already marked out by America.[49] To the circle of people around Horkheimer, America appears quite simply as an exceptionally favourable cognitive position from which to study not only America but the structures and tendencies of Western modernity as a whole. From that vantage point, solutions must be sought for the three excruciating puzzles that radical intellectuals have to face. Thus, *Dialectic of Enlightenment* aimed at 'nothing less than the discovery of why mankind, instead of entering into a truly human condition, is sinking into a new kind of barbarism.'[50] Horkheimer and Adorno had to come to terms

[46] Jäger 2004, 111.
[47] Adorno 2003, 65, 91, 190, 234, 322.
[48] Adorno 1969, 369.
[49] Ibid., 347.
[50] DoE, xi.

analytically with three experiences of intellectuals of their generation: namely, 'political disappointments at the absence of revolution in the West, the development of Stalinism in Soviet Russia, and the victory of fascism in Germany'.[51]

The certainty that the United States was the best observation post from which to answer these questions and to solve these puzzles rested upon the impression of US technological-industrial and military superiority over Europe. In retrospect, however, it is not so obvious that the certainty was justified. The United States itself never participated in at least two of the three great disappointments in question: fascism and Stalinism. Yet running throughout Adorno's work, including after his return to Germany, is a kind of mirror image of the position taken by Tocqueville. It is a mirror *image* to the extent that Adorno too is convinced that a perspective on America is a perspective on Europe's future. America is 'the most advanced bourgeois country, behind which the others hobble along'.[52] But it is a *reverse* image, because Adorno overwhelmingly – though not, as we shall see, consistently – believed that the conditions and trends visible in America were not progressive but catastrophic.

'It is rather the case that Europe, through the pull of its own development, is coming to resemble American conditions than that America is following the old continent.'[53] 'In all this, Europe is not ahead of America in a way that America might learn a tradition from it, but rather follows behind America.'[54] The first sense in which the United States is advanced, and therefore indicative of the future, is that class conflicts have been pacified there because no class consciousness has taken shape. 'In the advanced capitalist countries, the subjective class consciousness that has always been lacking in America may become toned down.'[55] Another significant pointer is in the field of youth culture and

[51] Habermas 1987, 116.
[52] Adorno, 'Theorie der Halbbildung', GS 8, 107.
[53] Adorno, 'Einführung in die Darmstädter Gemeindestudie', GS 20.2, 615.
[54] Adorno, 'Über Tradition', GS 10.1, 311.
[55] Adorno, 'Gesellschaft', GS 8, 15.

generational conflict: 'In this respect, as in many others, the younger generation in Germany will probably draw closer to American structures.'[56] The same is true of higher education and relations between students and teachers: 'There is also a discernible structural change in how students relate to university professors. As it has long been the case in America, where such processes are much starker than over here, the professor is gradually – but, I would say, inexorably – becoming a seller of knowledge, a little pitied because he is incapable of making that knowledge better serve his own material interests.'[57] As to the narrower field of the culture industry: 'The belief that the barbarity of the culture industry is a result of "cultural lag", of the fact that the American consciousness did not keep up with the growth of technology, is quite wrong. It was pre-fascist Europe which was backward relative to the trend towards monopolistic mass culture.'[58]

The crux of Adorno's critique of that advanced world of social modernization is a negative and totalizing concept of *equality*, not at all unlike that which Tocqueville developed in his most sombre observations on life in the New World and its acquisitive individualism. The sign of the age that can be read in American society is a compulsion to uniformity, understood as intolerance of deviation and, in the extreme case (for Adorno, always 'Auschwitz'), the violent extermination of 'difference'. 'When you go to America everywhere looks the

---

56 Adorno, 'Zum gegenwärtigen Stand der deutschen Soziologie', GS 8, 524.
57 Adorno, 'Tabus über den Lehrberuf', GS 10.2, 662 – a tendency on which his judgement is diametrically opposed to that of Max Weber. In a later work, when, as we shall see, Adorno's image of America had taken on a thoroughly positive coloration, we read: 'The old student ties to authority are unquestionably breaking down as the academic system draws closer to American forms, in a process that probably obeys immanent laws of society and should by no means be written off as a superficial Americanization' ('Zur Demokratisierung der deutschen Universitäten', GS 20.1, 334f.). This evaluation is evidently congruent with Max Weber's often-quoted remarks on conditions in American universities.
58 DoE, 132; translation modified.

same. The standardization, a product of technology and monopoly, is alarming. You think that qualitative differences have disappeared from life in as real a sense as the advance of rationality is eradicating them in the realm of method.'[59]

Under the pressure to conform, subjects are robbed of their subjectivity. 'In American, "he's quite a character" means the same as comical figure, queer fellow, poor chap.'[60] Differences that are still permitted are illusory and instrumentalized.[61] Deviance is the mere confirmation of a normality whose standards strictly circumscribe the degree of admissible deviation. The authors of *Dialectic of Enlightenment* illustrate this pseudo-individualism with the striking image of a key for the (then newly introduced) 'Yale lock': 'The defiant reserve or elegant appearance of the individual on show is mass-produced like Yale locks, whose only difference can be measured in fractions of millimetres.'[62] It is the minimal deviation of one key from all other keys that makes it suitable to be a key *like* all others. Similarly, the world of commodity exchange attains its totality through the fact that things sometimes happen as if the exchange principle had been suspended:

> In bringing cultural products wholly into the sphere of commodities, radio does not try to dispose of its culture goods themselves as commodities straight to the consumer. In America it collects no fees from the public, and so has acquired the illusory form of disinterested, unbiased authority which suits fascism admirably. The radio becomes the universal mouthpiece of the Führer.[63]

For Adorno, the scientistic branch of the culture industry is quantitative-empirical social research, whose methods require

[59] Adorno, 'Amorbach', GS 10.1, 304.
[60] Adorno, 'Zum Verhältnis von Soziologie und Psychologie', GS 8, 68. To interpolate an observation of my own, the expression 'This is a free country' is still today used with a shrug of the shoulders to answer a non-conformist view: it is a more polite version of 'You're an idiot.'
[61] See 'The Schema of Mass Culture', in Adorno 1991, esp. 67ff.
[62] DoE, 154. Cf. ibid., 145: 'Now any person signifies only those attributes by which he can replace everybody else: he is interchangeable, a copy.'
[63] DoE, 159.

abstraction from what he calls 'qualitative' differences; it treats the latter as something that does not deserve attention. 'The disparity between the colossal amount of material and the actually acquired knowledge is the mere result of abortive development, if not of . . . "Americanism", whose symptoms pervade empirical social research simply because it flourishes in America.'[64]

> The peculiar situation of empirical social research, in the narrow sense of the term, is bound up with the fact that it is not really rooted in the old *universitas litterarum*. It is closer than any other science to American pragmatism. Its origins in market research, and the fact that its technicians are largely cut to commercial and administrative purposes, are not extraneous aspects. It acquires – if I may avail myself of Max Scheler's shorthand expressions – power knowledge instead of formative knowledge.[65]

Thus, like all other forms of totalizing equalization, the cognitive elimination of qualitative differences that is promoted by empirical social research should be explained in terms of the valorization compulsion and the exchange principle. That principle leaves nothing and no one untouched, not even children, as Adorno notes in *Minima Moralia*: 'In America, . . . no child of even well-off parents has inhibitions about earning a few cents by newspaper rounds, and this nonchalance has found its way into the demeanour of adults.'[66]

First in the American writings of the 1940s,[67] then in a major lecture of 1959,[68] Adorno develops the concept of 'half-cultivation' to describe the effect of the culture industry and the quantitative social research enlisted in its service. Its characteristics include a paranoid fear of strangers and non-conformists, collective narcissism and a wish to 'belong'.[69]

---

64 Adorno, 'Teamwork in der Sozialforschung', GS 8, 494.
65 Adorno, 'Zur gegenwärtigen Stellung der empirischen Sozialforschung', GS 8, 491.
66 Adorno 1978, 195.
67 See DoE, 195f.
68 Adorno, 'Theorie der Halbbildung', GS 8, 93ff.
69 Ibid., 114.

Already in the *Briefe an die Eltern,* however, and in writings
from the late 1950s and after, Adorno suddenly makes a series
of markedly positive statements concerning America at the
micro-level of direct interaction at work and in everyday life.
These remarks record pleasant surprises, as it were, which are
hard to reconcile with the totalizing theory of the culture
industry and the post-liberal society of total marketization:
for example, that Americans by birth are 'more open-minded,
and above all more helpful, than European immigrants'.[70]
He also praises the academic type of 'cooperation in a democratic spirit', the 'most fruitful thing [he] became acquainted
with in America'.[71] The 'ostentatious positivity'[72] of these
judgements grew even stronger in the 1960s and is reflected
in the essay from 1968 on his 'academic experiences in
America'. This revaluation of American social conditions
must surely also be read as a message, which is meant to
convey his objection to the sharp criticisms of America then
current in the student protest movement.

But that would be too superficial an explanation, as would
the idea that his change of orientation stemmed from a sense
of loyalty to Horkheimer's marked pro-Americanism.[73] For,
in the 1950s and 1960s, Adorno deeply and successfully
involved himself in the tasks of extra-academic political
education. The theory of 'half-cultivation' was, so to speak,
filtered from its original 'culture industry' context and taken
up as a challenge to complete that very 'half-cultivation'
through energetic efforts in the field of politics. The 'constraints of the social system' now appeared to him as capable
of practical-pedagogic relativization.[74] In the essay 'Was ist
deutsch?', for example, we read: 'The energetic will to build
a free society, instead of just anxiously thinking about

[70] Adorno 1969, 350.
[71] Ibid., 358.
[72] Söllner 2003.
[73] On this see Albrecht et al. 2000.
[74] 'World history itself . . . appears not to allow its subjects the time
    in which everything might become better by itself. This relates

freedom or even reducing it in thought to voluntary subordination, does not lose what is good about it because the social system erects barriers to its realization.'[75] Adorno played a highly successful role in helping the 'latecomer nation' (H. Plessner) to close the gap through education:

> The fact that democracy came too late to Germany (that is, did not temporally coincide with the high era of economic liberalism) and was introduced by the victors has scarcely left untouched the relationship of the nation to itself. This is seldom directly expressed, because meanwhile things have been going well under democracy and it would conflict in political alliances with the institutionalized community of interests with the West (especially America). But the rancour against re-education speaks plainly enough. Indeed, one may say that in Germany the system of political democracy is accepted as what Americans call a 'working proposition', which has so far permitted or even promoted prosperity. But democracy has not become so established that people really experience it as their own cause and know themselves to be subjects of the political process.[76]

Adorno's political-pedagogic commitment led to numerous lectures and essays in large-circulation periodicals, and ironically also to many lectures on the radio, the medium that he had regarded in America with culture-critical suspicion. Political conditions in the United States and its democratic system now served more and more as yardstick and model for the messages that he tried to convey in the political education of Germany's postwar generation:

> Perhaps nowhere else is the difference between the political climate in America and Germany more visible. For the American the state is seen by its citizens as a form of social organization, never as an authority floating above the lives of individuals and

---

directly to democratic pedagogy' ('Was bedeutet: Aufarbeitung der Vergangenheit?', GS 10.2, 568).
[75] Adorno, 'Auf die Frage: Was ist deutsch?', GS 10.2, 697.
[76] From the highly influential essay 'Was bedeutet: Aufarbeitung der Vergangenheit?', GS 10.2, 559.

issuing orders to them, and still less as an absolute power. The absence of the officialdom so characteristic of European states, and especially the non-existence of a civil service with lifelong job security and all the ideas that go with it, are two of the things that most strike an immigrant to America.[77]

The social theory based on *Dialectic of Enlightenment* that Adorno developed with the material from his US experiences, as well as the pedagogic-journalistic activity that is anything but consistent with it and that its originators tried to use as a practical way out of the aporia of their ultra-radical 'self-overcoming ideology critique',[78] are generally recognized as having had a powerful influence on intellectual trends in the early Federal Republic.[79] After Adorno's return, then – and here we come to the question of the consistency of his image of America in his work – the 'vision of horror of an unavoidable coercive system'[80] underwent extensive and, above all, completely silent revision. Under Horkheimer's strategic guidance, two conceptual and political reorientations now decisively modified the picture of US society that he had formed in the 1940s.

First, the resigned, melancholic image of the message in a bottle, which had suggested that the critical intellect had no practical perspective and no addressee capable of political action, was modified and brightened up to such an extent that, from the early 1950s, the work of the Institute for Social Research and its members concentrated on university teaching, educational reform and academic organization (with a view to creating an amazingly inclusive social science network),[81] activity for the media and in adult education, the formation of intellectual elites, as well as the whole field of

---

[77] Adorno, 'Individuum und Staat', GS 20.1, 290f.
[78] Habermas 1987, 118.
[79] See Albrecht et al. 2000.
[80] Jäger 2004, 123.
[81] For example, Adorno maintained respectful professional and personal relations with Arnold Gehlen, the philosopher who had been close to the Nazi regime.

political-cultural socialization and education.[82] The general theme of these academic and media activities was, through 'detailed study' of the German past,[83] to prevent a relapse into the barbarity of National Socialism and, above all, its discreet removal or repression from the memory of contemporaries. This approach is clearly suited to the cultural and social-psychological interpretation of National Socialism,[84] which should be understood in terms of the mass emergence and constant virulence of 'authoritarian personalities' and 'not so closely linked to political-economic categories'.[85]

Second, on his way back from exile in America, as it were, Adorno arrived at a striking (if altogether implicit) revaluation of American democracy and society, which thereafter – in keeping with the re-education policy of the US occupation forces[86] and especially the emerging conditions of Cold War – became the normative model for the work of the institute. The orientation to American politics, society and culture was now the effective means for 'German pedagogy' to drain away the 'anti-civilizational, anti-Western undercurrent of the German heritage'.[87] For the task of 'educating the educators', Adorno completely turned away from his earlier verdict on 'administrative research' and even recommended 'what the Americans call behavioural sciences'.[88]

During the exile in California, America was experienced and theorized as the harbinger (or a mere variant) of totalitarian reification. But, looking back from Frankfurt at his

[82] See Albrecht et al. 2000; Demirovic 1999.
[83] Adorno, 'Was bedeutet: Aufarbeitung der Vergangenheit?', GS 10.2, 555–72.
[84] See Tenbruck 2000.
[85] Adorno, 'Was bedeutet: Aufarbeitung der Vergangenheit?', GS 10.2, 561.
[86] 'It had become clear that if it was to return to Germany, the Institute for Social Research could count only on the goodwill of the American occupying power, with whom any conflict was therefore to be avoided' (Jäger 2004, 117).
[87] Adorno, 'Was bedeutet: Aufarbeitung der Vergangenheit?', GS 10.2, 565.
[88] Adorno, 'Schuld und Abwehr', GS 9.2, 144.

American experiences, Adorno developed a diametrically opposite picture of the United States as a beacon of civil freedom that Europe, and especially defeated Germany in its state of moral catastrophe, had to take and study as its model. As far as I am aware, however, Adorno never made a single statement casting light on this complete turnaround in his perceptions of America.

In 'Kultur und Culture', a lecture he gave in 1958,[89] Adorno did cast an illuminating backward glance at his time in the United States. Without making any explicit cut or perspectival change in the image of America that formed the backdrop to *Minima Moralia* and *Dialectic of Enlightenment*, he now replaced that image with aspects of American society that he evoked with surprising sympathy.[90] America is 'a pure country of the bourgeois revolution' which, already as such, is normatively worthy of being preferred to the old continent and its residue of feudal and absolutist tradition, especially to Germany with its failed revolutions and belated modernization. The German intellectual culture of 'inwardness protected by power' (Thomas Mann) stands in contrast to the cheerful materialism of America's affluent society, a Cockaigne utopia of 'supermarkets' in which people (apart from those he has read about in 'the great American novelists', who write 'especially about the South') know neither

[89] The word 'culture', in English, actually does not appear once in the text of the lecture, but only in the title. Its main function is clearly to evade or revoke the opposition between (European) *Kultur* and (American) mere *Zivilisation* that had repeatedly inspired European anti-Americanism since the time of Kürnberger's pamphlet; the claim that there is such an opposition is, on the A-scale, one of the indicators of authoritarian personality structures. See Pollock 1955. Adorno did not want 'to expose [himself] to the misunderstanding that [he] subscribed to that fatal antithesis of *Kultur* and culture' (GS 10.2, 697).

[90] Some key passages from the lecture were published in the *Süddeutsche Zeitung* magazine supplement (29 August 2003), together with introductory comments that hint at Adorno's 'relationship to America marked by respect and almost tenderness'. The result is 'a different view . . . of America, which he carefully veiled in his published writings.' See also Maase 2001.

hunger nor even fear. That 'utopia come true' sees the every-day prospering of a peaceful, non-aggressive, good-natured, friendly humanity of everyday life, in which 'despite the profit motive a great deal is still left for individual people.'[91] Adorno even outdoes the most optimistic passages in Tocqueville's *Democracy in America* and reminds us of Adam Smith's vision[92] of the civilizing effect of market society due to the 'sympathy' and 'fellow-feeling' it generates among its members: 'This universality of commerce also means that everyone is there for everyone else, and that no one is as hard-ened in himself and his narrow private interests as people are in our old Europe. The political form of democracy is infi-nitely closer there to people's everyday feelings.'[93] Later we read, in an implicit reference to Tocqueville, that 'the forms of parliamentary democracy reach down into every possible informal group, club, schoolroom and God knows what else', and that this associative culture of what we would today call 'civil society' makes 'the power of resistance to totalitarian currents greater in America' than in Europe. Adorno also finds a beneficial side to the pressure on Americans to conform – a phenomenon which, as he explicitly notes, was first observed by Tocqueville, and which in his earlier writings in America he had subjected to vitriolic criticism. Even the dictatorship of 'keep smiling' changes those who would oth-erwise have an 'ill-natured, grumpy countenance' and imparts to them a 'certain humanity'.[94] As a result, things are less authoritarian in America: the freedom of discussion is greater; people feel no blind obedience; and children are less repressed and are not beaten at school. Adorno evidently finds it deeply attractive that the elitist striving for 'greatness'

---

[91] Adorno, 'Kultur und Culture', GS 10.2, 250f.

[92] Smith 1982.

[93] Adorno, 'Kultur und Culture', GS 10.2, 251.

[94] Adorno is here drawn into Kant's theory of 'innocent illusion': 'Men are, one and all, actors – the more so the more civilized they are. . . . For if men keep on playing these roles, the real virtues whose semblance they have merely been affecting for a long time are gradually aroused and pass into their attitude or will' (Kant 1974, 30ff.).

and 'eternal works' is alien to people in the United States. Even the alignment brought about by the culture industry is far from solid: 'Today there are quite a lot of non-conformist American poets.' Adorno also now values, as a sign of a democratic way of life, the positivistic academic culture which requires teachers and students alike to produce empirical evidence for any factual claim: 'this has something healthy . . . in comparison with a certain fondness for unruly thinking in Germany.' Altogether, then, in a diametrical reversal of his earlier judgement, it is with a sense of relief and confidence that Adorno identifies 'the overall historical trend to Americanization of Europe'. Were it not for the obsessive way in which he continues to write off jazz as aesthetically worthless, there would be no limit in his eyes to the superiority of American 'culture' over European '*Kultur*'.[95]

The thesis that America has a 'greater power of resistance to totalitarian currents' simply does not fit with the claim in the culture industry chapter of *Dialectic of Enlightenment* that such currents actually gained the upper hand there in American politics, economics and culture. Adorno the dialectician here forgoes the intellectual effort that might have clarified why both his positions are valid: he could have argued, as Tocqueville showed before him, that American virtues offer a possible remedy to the American dangers. Whereas Sombart in 1906 discussed why there was 'no socialism' in the United States, the critical theorists of the 1940s, in their diagnoses of the times, clearly did not tackle the obvious enough question of why a fascist movement had far less chance than a socialist movement of capturing shares of state power in the United States, and why instead of both there had been the New Deal.[96] The unsolved puzzle of American

[95] Adorno, 'Kultur und Culture', GS 10.2, 254ff.
[96] In their whole problematic, the major study of the 'authoritarian personality' conceived under Adorno's direction rests on the premiss that, for social-psychological reasons and under the impact of the culture industry, a fascist development in the United States is at least not to be ruled out. Otherwise, it would have made no sense to expend such a great research effort on the sources of this tendency.

ambivalence cannot have escaped Adorno's notice, but he lets it rest without comment.

The unresolved doubts at issue do become visible, however, in the 'foreword' that he attached to the published version of his 'Kultur und Culture' lecture (having failed in his efforts to prevent its appearance in print). The book containing this lecture is certainly a somewhat marginal yet perfectly normal edition – not, as the author pretends, a 'private printing' outside the framework of the book trade. And, whereas he quite regularly pressed for publication of his lectures in newspapers and journals, and subsequently in volumes of a Suhrkamp paperback series, he resisted in this exceptional case 'the behaviour of the administered world' that seeks to fix the 'fleeting word' in print. Indeed, he tells the reader that he cannot 'take responsibility for what is printed here', in order to 'avoid misinterpretations to which he would otherwise inevitably expose himself'.[97]

It may be seen from this relatively tiny portion of Adorno's work that the author was less convincing than his two predecessors, Tocqueville and Weber, in conceptually mastering the ambiguities of his American experiences and the conclusions that followed in comparison with European trends. Instead of the mutual restrictions and corrections between 'liberty' and 'equality' in Tocqueville's analysis of America, and instead of the ambivalence of Americanization, Europeanization and mediations between them that we find in Weber, Adorno offers *two* pictures of America that simply do not go together and are each as unconvincing as the other.

---

[97] Adorno, 'Kultur und Culture', GS 10.2, 246.

5

The United States in the Twenty-First Century: Traditions of Religious Socialization and Struggle against 'Evil'

If we now compare the comparisons that Tocqueville, Weber and Adorno make concerning the differences and convergences between the United States and Europe, we find a number of contrasts as well as areas of common ground. As far as the contrasts are concerned, I would like to return to the schema of diagnostic results and expectations that I presented in the introduction. These diagnoses may be constructed so that America is in a positive sense ahead of Europe (A1) or so that, in an equally positive sense, it preserves forces and inspirations that have been exhausted or submerged in the old continent (B1). But there is also the image of America as a negative avant-garde, in which the bad future of an 'Americanized' Europe can be read (A2), as well as the negative image of America as a crude, still uncivilized, culturally and institutionally backward social structure, to which a Europe conscious of its own more valuable traditions may be contrasted (B2). It is this latter image of innate defects or evils that have not yet been overcome, this stereotype of a crude, infantile or backward American society prone to regression and driven by inordinate acquisitiveness, that constitutes the essence of modern anti-Americanism. For this stereotype, Hegel,[1] with his

[1] See Hegel 1956.

Eurocentric deprecation of America as a bourgeois society lacking state or history, provides a 'lineage' or model 'operating beneath the surface' down to the present day.[2] Our three authors, on the other hand, for all the ambivalence of their analyses and judgements concerning the United States, fit remarkably closely the other three positions in the schema. Tocqueville's image of America unmistakably belongs to type A1: whatever his doubts and fears, he admires America as a vanguard model of society which, precisely because of its 'lack of roots', is 'a hundred times happier than our own'.[3] Max Weber's image of America just as clearly belongs to type B1, since he is full of admiration (though also pessimistic about the lasting viability) as he traces the sources of energy in American society represented by puritan sects and their voluntarist ethic of freedom. He praises the 'most massive originality' of life in American society,[4] its 'youthfully fresh and confident energy for good',[5] and – as far as 'genuine Yankeedom' is concerned – a 'superiority in the struggle for existence' that rests upon these residues.[6] For Weber, 'the average member of an American sect . . . stands far above the "Christians" of our national church',[7] because this 'sect man' (or else, 'Yankeedom')[8] has 'still' preserved a degree of autonomy and responsibility without any parallel in Europe. Finally, Adorno's experiences in and statements about America – at least those of the 1940s – clearly belong to type A2, which might be conceived in terms of an 'advance towards our decay'. From the United States, the 'most advanced observation

[2] Diner 2002, 21.
[3] Letter to Chabrol, 9 June 1831, quoted from Jardin 1988, 116–17.
[4] 'Science as a Vocation', in Weber 1958d, 149; translation modified.
[5] Marianne Weber 1975, 302; translation modified.
[6] Kaesler 2004.
[7] Letter to Adolf Harnack, 5 February 1906, Weber, *Gesamtausgabe*, II/5, 33.
[8] Weber, 'Sects', 311.

post',[9] he thinks he can register the 'destructiveness of progress' in the direction of the culture industry and the 'administered world' – a destructiveness already apparent in America itself and expected to spread everywhere else.

If we now consider the common ground in the three authors' otherwise so different images of America, or in the considerations on Europe that they developed in America, we are struck by their perception of the open-minded, trusting, egalitarian, cooperative and emotionally warm everyday culture of Americans. Of course, the three travellers to the United States theorize in very different ways the observation that American society – in its work life, neighbourly relations and system of clubs and associations – is liberally endowed with a 'social capital' that is lacking among Europeans. For Tocqueville, as we have seen, the proficiency of Americans in the 'art of association' and the 'habits of the heart' that serve them so well is the explanatory key, as well as the guarantee, for the fact that anomic phenomena do not destroy their society of individualist acquisitiveness and competition. He praises the robustness of a kind of 'micro-republican' ethic, which Weber was still able to observe (for example, in the *Liebeskommunismus*[10] practised by sects and associations), though at a stage of decline and deformation governed by private interests. Finally, Adorno describes the same phenomena – first in the *Briefe an die Eltern*, then more distinctly in the 'Kultur und Culture' lecture and his later retrospective in 'Scientific Experiences of a Scholar in America' – but he completely forgoes any historical or theoretical categorization of these social virtues and the conditions for their emergence; he simply records them, in the tone in which one takes note of a pleasant surprise.

I would like to conclude by raising the following question. Of the explanations, expectations and prognoses that our three authors made in relation to their observations in America and differences with European social conditions,

[9] Adorno 1969, 369.
[10] ES, 582.

which ones *no longer* stand up at all in the light of the present day? This test undertaken with the privilege of hindsight, which naturally does not mean that any demonstrable defect of explanation or prognosis can be blamed on a lack of scientific effort on the author's part, should serve here merely to indicate that a change has taken place since the time of their respective observations in both parts of the world, Europe and America, and especially in the relationship between the two.

With regard to Tocqueville, the effectiveness of mechanisms in America to correct the acquisitive individualism unleashed in the name of 'equality' is today less evident than it may have been at the time of his observations. Since the Second World War there have been numerous major studies in American social science – from David Riesman through Daniel Bell to Robert Putnam – which have given substance to such doubts. And, at least since America entered the First World War, Tocqueville's point about the relative unimportance of the military has had no foundation. Weber's prevailing view that American capitalism is likely to become 'Europeanized' in its post-heroic phase, through such developments as class-based political cleavages, statist-bureaucratic political conditions and neo-feudal structures, has not been confirmed in any way. And Adorno, in the last decade of his life, thoroughly (if rather casually) revised and toned down the theory of culture industry and authoritarian personality with which he had sought to update and radicalize Tocqueville's earlier insights.

This brings us to what I see as the decisive need for revision and updating in relation to trends in the second half of the twentieth century. All three of our authors implicitly start from the assumption that the civilized world of 'the West' is subject to the same evolutionary laws, and therefore to an ideal type of development constituted by common structural conditions; an understanding of these is then meant to help us identify deviations, advances, setbacks and breaks, but also, and especially, common features of a general process of Atlantic modernization. Among the things shared on both

sides of the North Atlantic are the dominant role of
Christianity, the experiences and consequences of revolutionary change in the last quarter of the eighteenth century,
the interconnection of science, technology, industry and prosperity, and the fact that at least the first waves of migration
to the United States came from Europe. Of course, these
common features – which also include the American special
relationship with Britain and the military role of the United
States in deciding the outcome of two world wars – need to
be set against important differences, such as the sheer size of
America and its distance from Europe; its special interests
and alliances in Latin America and the Pacific; its qualities as
a multi-ethnic settler society that forced back and decimated
the indigenous population; the ever-present past of Afro-
American slaves; the much greater heterogeneity of the
population and the inequality of their life chances; the
extreme fragmentation of the federal political system, which
is unknown anywhere in Europe; the lack of political parties
in a European sense; the markedly 'non-European' structure
and extent of American cities; the absence of wars in the
twentieth century with neighbouring countries (if one leaves
aside the military expeditions against Cuba, Grenada,
Panama and Nicaragua); the lack of experience of fascist or
Stalinist regimes or mass movements; and the role of the
United States, in the second half of the twentieth century, as
the military and economic leader of 'the West'. I leave it open
here whether the family resemblances or the structural differences carry more weight in this profile of attributes. But
the idea that similar evolutionary forces are at work in
European countries and the United States – an idea shared
with different emphases by all three of our authors – loses
much of its plausibility in view of the differences I have just
enumerated. It therefore seems advisable to make a sceptical
examination – and, if necessary, a consistent deconstruction –
of the inclusive transatlantic concept of 'the West' and a
Western community of values and trajectories of social and
political development.

America's main difference today from Europe – and *a*

fortiori with individual European countries – is that it is the architect and practically uncontrollable centre of an established global system of military, political, economic and ideological-cultural control. This means that any comparative investigation which assumes its objects to be separate entities belonging to a common category will inevitably rebound as an inadequate or naive undertaking, since it fails to grasp what is distinctive about them. The peculiarity of the United States is that, because of its global presence and power, it is able to demand a kind of external sovereignty and monopoly of decision-making, which, in cases of conflict, are not seriously hampered by the restrictions and supranational regulations and factual constraints that apply to all other states. This novel position of the United States in the world system lies completely outside the theoretical and experiential horizon of the authors we have discussed. Since the time when they were writing, the United States has become 'distinctive': it is no longer meaningful to analyse and compare it as if it were simply one state or social system among others.

Trips to, or stays in, the United States have ceased to offer the kind of special cognitive opportunities or comparative perspectives that our three travellers rightly assumed to exist in their own time. One reason for this is that, quite apart from mass tourism, regular visits to the United States have today become a routine activity for members of many professional groups; another is that one no longer needs to *travel* there to learn about the nature of American values, interests and cultural patterns. For nearly all participants in the global system, and certainly for Europeans, the United States is no longer a spatially distant entity but a military, commercial and cultural *presence*, here and now, in a common space. American realities have in part become our reality 'on the spot'. The dollar exchange-rate, US government decisions and military operations have immediate global effects and global news value. Our daily work materials rest upon technical inventions and developments in the United States, and the distinctively 'American' arts of cinema and music dominate the world market in the entertainment industry. I know of no academic discipline in which other than American research results and publications provide the intellectual premises and paradigmatic yardsticks for research and teaching.[11] One might even reverse Hegel's Hamburg–Altona metaphor for the relationship between Europe and America and see Europe today in the role of 'Altona'.

Furthermore, since the Second World War, American hegemony and dependence on America have led large parts of the world to emulate the United States. 'America' has become geographically deterritorialized, especially since the demise of Soviet-controlled state socialism. It was therefore not laws of development derived from the pioneering case of America, but rather the political-military, economic and cultural-ideological supremacy of the United States which led other countries in the twentieth century to draw closer in many ways to the US model – not only because they freely chose American conditions as a model of social development and imitated its institutions (for example, federalism or the presidential system), but also because the geographically diffuse superpower imperiously suggested that they adopt its models of economic life, politics and culture. Over large areas, American influence worked in many respects to the clear advantage of those who landed in its gravitational field after the Second World War. In any event, members of my generation felt it as an unmixed blessing that the United States played in Europe the military, political, cultural and economic role that it did during and after the Second World War. But this only underlines the distinctiveness and near-global presence of the United States, which became through such developments a power beyond all comparison.

The great majority of countries on earth are today either allied with and dependent on the United States for their military security or potentially threatened by its military power. For this reason, it is not an extravagant ambition but an

---

[11] Were there to be a research area to which this did not apply, its leading representatives would immediately be courted with irresistible offers from elite American universities.

accurate account of the facts if the United States describes itself as the power responsible for global order. Since the First World War it has been part of the American identity to project itself outwards on to others – as if, to confirm that identity in their own eyes, Americans found it important to shape others in their own image, and thus to gain admiring and grateful recognition, to win 'hearts and minds'. For this purpose, and not at all only for economic reasons, Americans acted overseas (and in their own southern 'backyard', from the Rio Grande to Tierra del Fuego) to uphold and gain recognition for 'freedom and democracy', seeing the fight for those values by 'traditionless' America as the heart of their own identity. It is not only the current US administration that pursues the self-given mission of 'making the world a better place' *manu militari*; behind this mission we can see an identity-building obsession, through which the inner cracks of American society are covered up with military means directed towards the outside world. Another peculiarity of today's United States that sharply contrasts with the three authors' findings is the fact that it is the only country which can, in the case of claimed necessity, treat external rules, principles and agreements as non-binding; it does not, as President George W. Bush so aptly put it, need to 'seek a permission slip' from anyone,[12] simply because no one could effectively forbid it to do anything it wanted. In case of necessity, so its current leadership appears to believe, the United States can command recognition of its brute power from all other participants in the international system, and thereby drop claims for moral authority without suffering any harmful consequences.[13]

The sovereign failure to comply with an *external* standard

---

[12] 'America Will Never Seek a Permission Slip', State of the Union Address, 20 January 2004.

[13] It is another question – which cannot be discussed here – whether, on what conditions (military, commercial, etc.) and against whom the unilateral deployment of American sovereignty might prove to be an unwise form of conduct detrimental to America's own interests.

of legitimation required of all other countries – for example, the rules and institutions of international law and various agreements on trade and the environment, as well as the simple obligation to give the public truthful information – can be compensated on only one condition: if it is *internally* legitimated by the defence of American interests and values. This condition is met if a religious justification can be adduced for national interests, through recourse to the religious foundations of American social integration that were already identified by Tocqueville and Weber. That which is not covered by earthly justice must be presented as the execution of God's will; the more meagre the formal justifications for war, the more urgent it becomes to make it 'holy'. Indeed, it was with precisely this shift that the President ended his State of the Union address in 2004: 'The cause we serve is right, because it is the cause of all mankind. The momentum of freedom in our world is unmistakable – and it is not carried forward by our power alone. We can trust in that greater power who guides the unfolding of the years. And in all that is to come, we can know that His purposes are just and true.'

This strangely unilateral universalist project of bringing order and freedom to the world and thereby securing American society from outside attack – a project that may even recommend itself as altruistic – has two indispensable preconditions. First, it must be impossible to attack America itself, either politically or ideologically through the questioning of American values, or militarily through a challenge to the territorial integrity of the United States. The only power that can aspire to a global leadership role is one which is able by nature to operate from an unassailable fortress, immune from loss of its power through internal division or external force. And, as Tocqueville already saw, the natural laws of geography have protected the United States from any conceivable strategic defeat, so that it has the blessing of zero risk to its own territory, which can also be secured through major technological projects such as the development of anti-ballistic missiles. Consequently, military risks are asymmetrically distributed from the very outset, and the price of defeat will always be paid by the enemy. Victory will unquestionably go to the United States, which may have to cope with material losses and human casualties and, in extreme cases, even military disgrace (as in the attempted invasion of Cuba at the Bay of Pigs), tactical defeats (Pearl Harbor) or lost wars in distant continents (Vietnam), but never has to face the risk that any other belligerent assumes to be an obvious possibility in war: the loss of parts of its national territory, national population or national system of rule.

The logic of deterrence during the Cold War served to guarantee this asymmetry. So long as the adversary was a state or military alliance whose leadership, under conditions of 'mutually assured destruction', was rational enough to avoid making its potential threat a reality, an attack on the territory of the United States remained outside the bounds of the conceivable. The significance of 11 September 2001 – and this was the aim of the terrorists' vilely executed plan – is precisely that the assurance of being safe from attack and losses on one's own territory was rudely shattered before the eyes of the world.

On the other hand, the project of continually basing global control on American foundations stands or falls with the claim that certain powers in the world are 'rogue states' or part of an 'axis of evil' or non-state perpetrators of violence. The connection between the two is clear. Since America has no enemies that pose a serious threat, it needs to have 'evil' enemies. The wars, or 'crusades', against them are meant to end not with surrender and a peace settlement, but rather with the final eradication of evil. Thus, the unambiguous negativity of the enemy is supposed to call forth the voluntary solidarity of friends, with such an inexorable logic that the invincibility of the leading power of the 'Free World' (or at least in a 'coalition of the willing' cobbled together through the selective use of carrots and sticks) becomes an ever more solidly established certainty. If such 'evil' enemies did not exist, the universalist claim to be looking after the freedom and welfare of global society would immediately collapse amid ridicule – or arouse the suspicion that the 'new world order' was about nothing other than an imperial *pax Americana*.[14] America needs the assurance of its own invincibility; and it needs enemies who can be depicted as morally deserving of attack on the grounds that they are representatives of 'evil'.

Since the collapse of the Soviet Union, the United States has had a largely free hand in selecting these 'evil' enemies, who have to face a rich panoply of commercial and military sanctions. These enemies are defined by one or more of three attributes: they support, harbour or assist (actively or by default) people engaged in 'terrorism'; they dispose of, or are seeking to acquire, weapons of mass destruction; and they operate a violently repressive regime against all or part of their own population.[15] However, 'rogue state' and 'terrorist' are highly flexible labels, both theoretically and practically. If necessary, lies and deception can be used to suggest that a country possesses or has the potential to develop weapons of mass destruction (Iraq, Cuba), and in other cases real evidence of the same can be opportunistically ignored (Pakistan). States that only allegedly have a WMD potential then become the target for preventive (or, in a logically monstrous intensification, 'pre-emptively preventive') intervention. Similarly, the criterion of 'terrorism', or state sponsorship and support for terrorism, is wide open to interested definitions and can also be disregarded for opportunistic reasons – quite apart from the fact that the emergence of violent non-state actors seeking to gain power ('terrorists') is often not so much a legitimating cause as a factual consequence of military intervention that leads to the destruction of existing state

---

[14] The course and outcome of the Vietnam War showed how difficult things become for the leading power when doubts are raised, both domestically and among important external partners, as to the moral repulsiveness and political danger of the chosen enemy. This problem obviously did not arise in the case of the Kosovo War, coming as it did after the Srebrenica massacre.

[15] See Mann 2003.

structures (Iraq).[16] The repressiveness of a state appears to be the most plausible criterion of its 'evil' character, but this clearly plays the least significant role in American policy; one thinks here of that 'other' 11 September (in Chile, 1973), when a regime bent on large-scale killing of its own population was not brought down by US foreign policy but helped to power and given favourable support. Yet the superpower has a completely free hand in defining the 'evil enemy' only if it can successfully bypass the authority of others (e.g. the UN Security Council) to construct such definitions and manipulate the national and international public with false claims to certainty.

The end of the Cold War in November 1989 brought the surprising and definitive self-liquidation of the enemy of the time – a system which, at least in one dominant reading, had reliably qualified as an enemy in the postwar decades according to two of the three criteria mentioned above (internal repression and assumed external aggressiveness). There is little dispute about the repressive and aggressive character of the Iraqi regime that was bombed out of existence in 2003. But it was not unimportant whether this verdict on the regime remained a matter for the American government and sections of international public opinion, or whether it was validated in a UN Security Council resolution that explicitly made it the basis for certain sanctions. Today there is scarcely any realistic prospect of successful nation-building in Iraq. Rather, American action there has created the ideal conditions for the new 'terrorist' enemy, who is known to flourish as nowhere else in the kind of state ruins to which American bombing reduced the country both physically and metaphorically. It is true that, at least in the eyes of the public in the liberal democracies, the criterion regarding the morally

---

[16] In March 2003, in the run-up to the Iraq War, the US administration claimed more than once that there was a base for terrorist groups or activities inside Iraq. It is only since the (official) end of the war, however, and as a direct result of it, that there have been unmistakable signs of such activities.

reprehensible nature of the new enemy is satisfied in Iraq more clearly than in any other case since the American war against Hitler's Germany and its allies. But in the 'new wars', in which a state or alliance of states is directly opposed to a network of non-state actors, one is literally talking of 'perennial' war that cannot be won by military means. Nor, given the lack of anyone empowered to sign the terms of surrender, can we imagine how it would be securely established that the war had actually come to an end.

References and Bibliography

Abraham, David, 1996, 'Liberty without Equality: The Property-Rights Connection in a "Negative Citizenship" Regime', *Law and Social Inquiry*, 21, 1, 1–65.

Adorno, Theodor W., 1958, 'Kultur und Culture', *Hessische Hochschulwochen für staatswissenschaftliche Fortbildung*, 23, 246–59.

Adorno, Theodor W., 1969, 'Scientific Experiences of a Scholar in America', in Donald Fleming and Bernard Bailyn (eds), *The Intellectual Migration: Europe and America, 1930–1960*. Cambridge, MA: Harvard University Press.

Adorno, Theodor W., 1978, *Minima Moralia: Reflections from Damaged Life*, trans. E. F. N. Jephcott. London: Verso.

Adorno, Theodor W., 1991, *The Culture Industry: Selected Essays on Mass Culture*, ed. J. M. Bernstein. London: Routledge.

Adorno, Theodor W., 1997, *Gesammelte Schriften*, ed. Rolf Tiedemann, Frankfurt am Main: Suhrkamp; abbreviated in notes to GS.

Adorno, Theodor W., 2003, *Briefe an die Eltern 1939–1951*, Frankfurt am Main: Suhrkamp.

Adorno, Theodor W., and Max Horkheimer, 2003, *Theodor W. Adorno/Max Horkheimer. Briefwechsel*, vol. 4.1. Frankfurt am Main: Suhrkamp.

Adorno, Theodor W., Else Frenkel-Brunswik, Daniel J. Levinson and R. Nevitt Sanford, 1969 [1950], *The Authoritarian Personality*. New York: Norton.

Albrecht, Clemens, Günter C. Behrmann, Michael Bock, Harald Homann and Friedrich H. Tenbruck, 2000, *Die intellektuelle Gründung der Bundesrepublik: Eine Wirkungsgeschichte der Frankfurter Schule*. Frankfurt am Main: Campus.

Bellah, Robert N., Richard Madson, William L. Sullivan, Ann Swidler and Steven M. Tipton, 1985, *Habits of the Heart: Individualism and Commitment in American Life*. Berkeley: University of California Press.

Benjamin, Walter, 2003, *Selected Writings*, vol. 4: *1938–1940*. Cambridge, MA: Harvard University Press.

Berger, Peter L., and Richard J. Neuhaus, 1996, *To Empower People: From State to Civil Society*. Washington, DC: AEI Press.

Busch, Alexander, 1959, *Die Geschichte des Privatdozenten: Eine soziologische Studie zur großbetrieblichen Entwicklung der deutschen Universitäten*. Stuttgart: Enke.

Claussen, Detlev, 2003, *Theodor W. Adorno. Ein letztes Genie*. Frankfurt am Main: Fischer.

Demirovic, Alex, 1999, *Der nonkonformistische Intellektuelle: Die Entwicklung der Kritischen Theorie zur Frankfurter Schule*. Frankfurt am Main: Suhrkamp.

Deutscher Bundestag, Enquête-Kommission 'Zukunft des Bürgerschaftlichen Engagements' (ed.), 2001, *Bürgerliches Engagement und Zivilgesellschaft*, Schriftenreihe vol. 1. Opladen: Leske & Budrich.

Diggins, John Patrick, 1996a, 'America's Two Visitors: Tocqueville and Weber', *La Revue Tocqueville/The Tocqueville Review*, 17, 2, 165–82.

Diggins, John Patrick, 1996b, *Max Weber: Politics and the Spirit of Tragedy*. New York: Basic Books.

Diner, Dan, 2002, *Feindbild Amerika: Über die Beständigkeit eines Ressentiments*. Berlin: Propyläen.

Eisermann, Gottfried, 1968, 'Max Weber und Amerika', in *Bedeutende Soziologen*. Stuttgart: Enke, 1–25.

Elster, Jon, 1993, *Political Psychology*. Cambridge: Cambridge University Press.

Feldhoff, Jürgen, 1967, *Die Politik der egalitären Gesellschaft: Zur soziologischen Demokratie-Analyse bei Alexis de Tocqueville*. Cologne and Opladen: Westdeutscher Verlag.

Freund, Dorrit, 1974, 'Max Weber und Alex de Tocqueville', *Archiv für Kulturgeschichte*, 457–64.

Galston, William A, 2000: 'Civil Society and the "Art of Association"', *Journal of Democracy*, 11, 1, 64–70.

Gneuss, Christian and Jürgen Kocka (eds), 1988, *Max Weber. Ein Symposium*. Munich: Deutscher Taschenbuchverlag.

Goethe, Johann Wolfgang von, 1958, *Goethes Werke*, ed. Reinhard Buchwald, 10 vols. Weimar: Volksverlag.

Habermas, Jürgen, 1983, 'Theodor Adorno: The Primal History of Subjectivity – Self-Affirmation Gone Wild', in *Philosophical-Political Profiles*, trans. Frederick G. Lawrence. London: Heinemann, 99–110.

Habermas, Jürgen, 1987, *The Philosophical Discourse of Modernity*, trans. Frederick G. Lawrence. Cambridge: Polity.

Habermas, Jürgen, 1989, *The Structural Transformation of the Public Sphere*, trans. Thomas Burger. Cambridge: Polity.

Haller, Gret, 2002, *Die Grenzen der Solidarität: Europa und die USA im Umgang mit Staat, Nation und Religion*. Berlin: Aufbau-Verlag.

Hamilton, Alexander, James Madison and John Jay, 1999[1787], *Federalist Papers*. New York: Mentor.

Hartmann, Martin, 2003, *Die Kreativität der Gewohnheit: Grundzüge einer pragmatistischen Demokratietheorie*. Frankfurtam Main: Campus.

Hecht, Martin, 1998, *Modernität und Bürgerlichkeit: Max Webers Freiheitslehre im Vergleich mit den politischen Ideen von Alexis de Tocqueville und Jean-Jacques Rousseau*. Berlin: Duncker & Humblot.

Hegel, Georg Wilhelm Friedrich, 1956, *Lectures on the Philosophy of History*, trans. J. Sibree. Rev. edn, New York: Dover.

Heller, Hermann, 1983 [1934], *Staatslehre*. 6th edn, Tübingen: Mohr.

Hennis, Wilhelm, 1988, 'Tocqueville's Perspective', *Interpretation*, 16, 1.

Hennis, Wilhelm, 1995, 'Freiheit durch Assoziation', *Frankfurter Allgemeine Zeitung*, 4 January.

Hennis, Wilhelm, 2000a, *Max Weber's Central Question*, trans. Keith Tribe. Newbury: Threshold Press.

Hennis, Wilhelm, 2000b, *Max Weber's Science of Man*, trans. Keith Tribe. Newbury: Threshold Press.

Holmes, Stephen, 1993, 'Manifold Lessons', in Wissenschaftskolleg zu Berlin, *Jahrbuch 1991/92*, Berlin: Nicolaische Verlagsbuch-handlung, 210–32.

Horkheimer, Max and Theodor W. Adorno, 1986, *Dialectic of Enlightenment*. London: Verso; abbreviated in notes to DoE.

Horkheimer, Max, Erich Fromm, Herbert Marcuse and Hans Mayer, 1987 [1936], *Studien über Autorität und Familie:*

Forschungsberichte aus dem Institut für Sozialforschung. Lüneburg: Klampen.

Howard, Marc M., 2003, *The Weakness of Civil Society in Post-Communist Europe*. Cambridge: Cambridge University Press.

Jäger, Lorenz, 2004, *Adorno: A Political Biography*, trans. Stewart Spencer. New Haven, CT, and London: Yale University Press.

Jardin, André, 1988, *Tocqueville: A Biography*, trans. Lydia Davis with Robert Hemenway. New York: Farrar Straus Giroux.

Joas, Hans, 1993, 'An Underestimated Alternative: America and the Limits of "Critical Theory"', in *Pragmatism and Social Theory*. Chicago: University of Chicago Press, 79–93.

Kaesler, Dirk, 2004, 'Bilder von Amerika'. Unpublished manuscript, Marburg.

Kagan, Robert, 2003, *Of Paradise and Power: America and Europe in the New World Order*. New York: Knopf.

Kalberg, Stephen, 2000, 'Tocqueville und Weber: Zu den soziologischen Ursprüngen der Staatsbürgerschaft – die politische Kultur der amerikanischen Demokratie', *Soziale Welt*, 51, 1, 67–86.

Kamphausen, Georg, 1991, 'Das Bekenntnis zur Selbstevidenz: Über das Verhältnis von Politik und Religion in den Vereinigten Staaten von Amerika', in Hans Thomas (ed), *Amerika – Eine Hoffnung, zwei Visionen*. Cologne: Bachem, 251–90.

Kamphausen, Georg, 2002, *Die Erfindung Amerikas in der Kulturkritik der Generation von 1890*. Weilerswist: Velbrück.

Kant, Immanuel, 1952 [1790], *The Critique of Judgement*, trans. James Creed Meredith. Oxford: Clarendon Press.

Kant, Immanuel, 1974 [1798], *Anthropology from a Pragmatic Point of View*, trans. Mary J. Gregor. The Hague: Martinus Nijhoff.

Kornhauser, William, 1959, *The Politics of Mass Society*. New York: Free Press.

Krüger, Christa, 2001, *Max und Marianne Weber*. Zurich: Pendo.

Lassman, Peter, 1993, 'Democracy and Disenchantment. Weber and Tocqueville on the "Road to Servitude"', in Herminio Martins (ed.), *Knowledge and Passion: Essays in Honor of John Rex*. London: I. B. Tauris.

Lipset, Seymour Martin, 1981, *Political Man: The Social Bases of Politics*. Baltimore: Johns Hopkins University Press.

Loader, Colin and Jeffrey C. Alexander, 1985, 'Max Weber on Churches and Sects in North America: An Alternative Path towards Rationalism', *Sociological Theory*, 3, 1, 1–6.

Locke, John, 1988 [1690], *Two Treatises of Government*, ed. Peter Laslett. Cambridge: Cambridge University Press.

Maase, Kaspar, 2001, '"Amerika" zwischen Hochkultur und Massenkultur', *Volkskunde Rheinland-Pfalz*, 16, 2, 2–12; http://www.volkskunde-rheinland-pfalz.de/seiten/zeitschrift/2001_02/0102_amerika. shtml.

Mann, Michael, 2003, *Incoherent Empire*. London: Verso.

Marx, Karl and Friedrich Engels, 1959–, *Werke*, ed. Institut für Marxismus-Leninismus beim ZK der SED. Berlin: Dietz.

Mill, John Stuart, 1974 [1863], *Utilitarianism*. New York: New American Library.

Mitzman, Arthur, 1971, *The Iron Cage: An Historical Interpretation of Max Weber*. New York: Universal Library.

Mommsen, Wolfgang J., 1974a, *The Age of Bureaucracy. Perspectives on the Political Sociology of Max Weber*. Oxford: Blackwell.

Mommsen, Wolfgang J., 1974b, *Max Weber: Gesellschaft, Politik und Geschichte*. Frankfurt am Main: Suhrkamp.

Mommsen, Wolfgang J., 1984, *Max Weber and German Politics 1890–1920*, trans. Michael Sternberg. Chicago: University of Chicago Press.

Morgenthau, Hans J., 1978, *Politics Among Nations: The Struggle for Power and Peace*. 5th rev. edn, New York: Knopf.

Müller-Doohm, Stefan, 2005, *Adorno: A Biography*. Cambridge: Polity.

Münkler, Herfried, 1993, *Thomas Hobbes*. Frankfurt am Main: Campus.

Pisa, Karl, 1984, *Alexis de Tocqueville, Prophet des Massenzeitalters: Eine Biographie*. Stuttgart: DVA.

Pollock, Friedrich, 1955, *Gruppenexperiment: Ein Studienbericht*. Frankfurt am Main: EVA.

Portinaro, Pier Paolo, 2001, 'Amerika als Schule der politischen Entzauberung: Eliten und Parteien bei Max Weber', in Edith Hanke and Wolfgang J. Mommsen (eds), *Max Webers Herrschaftssoziologie: Studien zur Entstehung und Wirkung*. Tübingen: Mohr Siebeck, 285–302.

Preuß, Ulrich K., 1990, *Revolution, Fortschritt und Verfassung: Zu einem neuen Verfassungsverständnis*. Berlin: Wagenbach.

Preuß, Ulrich K. (ed.), 1994, *Zum Begriff der Verfassung*. Frankfurt am Main: Fischer.

Putnam, Robert D., 1993, *Making Democracy Work: Civic Traditions in Modern Italy*. Princeton, NJ: Princeton University Press.

Putnam, Robert D., 2000, *Bowling Alone: The Collapse and Revival of American Community*. New York: Simon & Schuster.

Rabinbach, Anson, 1995, 'German-Jewish Connections: The New York Intellectuals and the Frankfurt School in Exile', *German Politics and Society*, 13, 3, 108–29.

Riesman, David, 1953, *The Lonely Crowd: A Study of the Changing American Character*. New York: Doubleday.

Rollmann, Hans, 1993, '"Meet Me in St. Louis": Troeltsch and Weber in America', in Hartmut Lehmann and Guenther Roth (eds), *Weber's 'Protestant Ethic': Origins, Evidence, Context*. Cambridge: Cambridge University Press, 357–83.

Roth, Guenther, 2001, *Max Webers deutsch-englische Familiengeschichte 1800–1950*. Tübingen: Mohr.

Rottweiler, Hektor [T. W. Adorno], 1936, 'Über Jazz', *Zeitschrift für Sozialforschung*, 5, 1, 235–59.

Scaff, Lawrence A., 1998, 'The "Cool Objectivity of Sociation": Max Weber and Marianne Weber in America', *History of Human Science*, 11, 2, 61–82.

Smith, Adam, 1982 [1759], *The Theory of Moral Sentiments*. Indianapolis: Liberty Classics.

Söllner, Alfons, 2003, 'Adornos Amerika', *Mittelweg 36*, 12, 4, 3–25.

Sombart, Werner, 1976 [1906], *Why Is There No Socialism in the United States?*, trans. Patricia M. Hocking and C. T. Husbands. London: Macmillan.

Tenbruck, Friedrich H., 2000, 'Von der verordneten Vergangenheitsbewältigung zur intellektuellen Gründung der Bundesrepublik: Die politischen Rahmenbedingungen', in C. Albrecht et al., *Die intellektuelle Gründung der Bundesrepublik*. Frankfurt am Main: Campus, 78–96.

Tocqueville, Alexis de, 1896 [1893], *The Recollections of Alexis de Tocqueville*, trans. Alexander Teixeira de Mattos. London: Henry & Co.

Tocqueville, Alexis de, 1945 [1835, 1840], *Democracy in America*, 2 vols., trans. Henry Reeve, rev. F. Bowen. New York: Vintage Books; abbreviated in notes to DiA.

Tocqueville, Alexis de, 1951–, *Œuvres complètes*, ed. Jacob Peter Mayer. Paris: Gallimard.

Tocqueville, Alexis de, 1988 [1856], *The Ancien Regime*, trans. John Bonner. London: Dent.

Todd, Emmanuel, 2003, *After the Empire: The Breakdown of American Order*. New York: Columbia University Press.

Weber, Marianne, 1975, *Max Weber: A Biography*, trans. Harry Zohn. New York: John Wiley & Sons.

Weber, Max, 1949, *The Methodology of the Social Sciences*, ed. Edward A. Shils and Henry A. Finch. New York: Free Press.

Weber, Max, 1952 [1904], 'Kapitalismus und Agrarverfassung', *Zeitschrift für die gesamte Staatswissenschaft*, 108, 431–52.

Weber, Max, 1958a, *Gesammelte Politische Schriften*. 2nd edn, Tübingen: Mohr; abbreviated in notes to GPS.

Weber, Max, 1958b, *The Protestant Ethic and the Spirit of Capitalism*, trans. Talcott Parsons. New York: Charles Scribner's & Sons; abbreviated in notes to PE.

Weber, Max, 1958c, 'The Protestant Sects and the Spirit of Capitalism', in *From Max Weber: Essays in Sociology*, ed. H. H. Gerth and C. Wright Mills. New York: Oxford University Press.

Weber, Max, 1958d, *From Max Weber: Essays in Sociology*, trans. and ed. H. H. Gerth and C. Wright Mills. New York: Oxford University Press.

Weber, Max, 1962, *Ancient Judaism*, ed. Don Martindale. New York: Free Press.

Weber, Max, 1968, *Gesammelte Aufsätze zur Wissenschaftslehre*. Tübingen: Mohr; abbreviated in notes to GAWL.

Weber, Max, 1978, *Economy and Society*, ed. Guenther Roth and Claus Wittich. Berkeley: University of California Press; abbreviated in notes to ES.

Weber, Max, 1980, *Wirtschaft und Gesellschaft*. Tübingen: Mohr.

Weber, Max, 1984–, *Gesamtausgabe*. Tübingen: Mohr.

Weber, Max, 1988a [1920], *Gesammelte Aufsätze zur Religionssoziologie*. Tübingen: Mohr; abbreviated in notes to GARS.

Weber, Max, 1988b, *Gesammelte Aufsätze zur Soziologie und Sozialpolitik*. Tübingen: Mohr; abbreviated in notes to SSP.

Weber, Max, 1994, *Weber: Political Writings*, ed. Peter Lassman and Ronald Speirs. Cambridge: Cambridge University Press.

Wiggershaus, Rolf, 1994, *The Frankfurt School: Its History, Theories and Political Significance*. Cambridge: Polity.

Wolin, Sheldon S., 2001, *Tocqueville between Two Worlds: The Making of a Political and Theoretical Life*. Princeton, NJ: Princeton University Press.

Index